EMPATHY UNLOCKED LEARNING TO CONNECT IN A DISCONNECTED WORLD

PRACTICAL TECHNIQUES FOR ATTENTIVE COMMUNICATION, UNDERSTANDING PERSPECTIVES, SELF-COMPASSION, AND SETTING BOUNDARIES

DELIA SIKES

NEEL MOUNTAIN PUBLISHING

Copyright © 2024 by Delia Sikes.

All rights reserved.

No portion of this book may be reproduced in any form without written permission from the publisher or author, except as permitted by U.S. copyright law.

Legal Notice:

This book is only for personal use. No one can amend, distribute, sell, use, quote or paraphrase any part of the content within this book without the consent of the author or publisher.

Disclaimer Notice:

Under no circumstances will any blame or legal responsibility be held against the publisher, or author, for any damages, reparation, or monetary losses, direct or indirect, due to the information contained within this book, including but not limited to errors, omissions, or inaccuracies. You are responsible for your own choices, actions, and results.

Please note the information contained within this document is for educational and entertainment purposes only. All effort has been expended to present accurate, up-to-date, complete and reliable information. No warranties of any kind are declared or implied. Readers acknowledge that the author is not engaging in the rendering of legal, financial, medical or professional advice. The content within this book has been derived from various sources. Please consult a licensed professional before attempting any techniques outlined in this book.

Contents

Introduction   1
1. What Is Empathy?   4
2. Use Practical Techniques for Attentive Communication   17
3. Recognize Diverse Perspectives   30
4. Focus on Self-Empathy and Self-Care Techniques   46
5. Set Healthy Boundaries   61
* Help Us Spread Empathy *   76
6. Lead with Empathy   78
7. Achieve Empathy in the Digital Age   94
8. Navigate Difficult Relationships   107
9. Commit to Empathy for Personal Growth   126
10. Explore Interactive Exercises and Practical Applications   144
Conclusion   164
References   168

INTRODUCTION

Recently, I found myself in a heated debate on social media about politics, a topic that had divided many. As I keyed my response, I suddenly realized I was not trying to understand the other person's perspective; I was trying to win the argument. That moment of reflection was jarring—it made me recognize just how easily we can sideline empathy in our quests to assert our viewpoints in the digital age.

This epiphany inspired the creation of this book. Its purpose is simple yet profound: to equip you with practical techniques for cultivating empathy. In a world where digital communication often substitutes for face-to-face interaction, fostering empathy is crucial. We need it to forge meaningful connections, to truly understand each other, and to navigate the complexities of modern life.

We're living in a time where empathy is diminishing. Research shows that people today are less empathic than 30 years ago. Studies have found that college students, for example, have shown a 40% decline in empathy over the past few decades. Several factors contribute to this decline, particularly in the digital age. The constant barrage of digital information can desensitize us to the actual emotional experiences of others. The pandemic forced us to use digital learning, work, and communication full-time, another contributing factor. At the same time, the brevity and impersonality of online communication often fail to convey the full human emotional spectrum. This lack of empathy is not just a personal issue; it affects our workplaces, communities, and relationships. Technology makes us more connected than ever, yet we often feel emotionally disconnected.

Do you feel the world is too divided for empathy to matter? It's not a hopeless cause. We're going to review real solutions for bridging gaps. Empathy can be a powerful tool for cutting through tension, building understanding, and creating connections in today's polarized world.

So, what is empathy? Empathy is the ability to understand and share another person's feelings. It is different from sympathy, which is feeling pity for someone else's misfortune, and distinct from compassion, which is a step further, involving a desire to help. For example, if a friend loses their job, you demonstrate empathy by genuinely feeling their stress and disappointment, sympathy by expressing sorrow for their situation, and compassion by actively helping them find new opportunities. Empathy is about truly seeing and hearing others, a skill we can develop with practice. This distinction is crucial as each response can shape our interactions differently.

In this book, we'll explore various facets of empathy. We'll start with the basics of empathetic communication, including active listening and understanding diverse perspectives. We'll also cover self-empathy and the importance of setting boundaries, especially when dealing with people who lack empathy. We'll dive into how empathy functions in the workplace, balancing it with objectivity and using it as a leadership skill. Each chapter will provide practical techniques and real-life examples to help you apply these concepts.

The book includes a quiz, three worksheets, three leadership case studies, and 118 guided exercises to make this journey interactive and engaging. These tools are designed to help you practice and internalize what you learn. They will enable you to assess your current level of empathy, identify areas for improvement, and track your progress over time.

Allow me to introduce myself. My name is Delia Sikes, and I have spent years learning about communication barriers and the power of empathy. My passion for this subject stems from personal experiences, including dealing with relatives who struggled with empathy. These experiences have driven me to help others overcome similar challenges and achieve meaningful connections.

What can you expect to gain from this book? By the end, I hope you will have enhanced your empathic communication skills, be better equipped to handle personal and professional relationships, and have the tools to manage empathy in various contexts, from virtual meetings to social media interactions. Most importantly, you will be on a path to becoming a more empathic and connected individual.

I invite you to commit to this journey of learning and applying empathy. It won't always be easy, but the rewards are immense. Empathy has the power to transform your relationships, your work environment, and your overall sense of well-being. Together, let's unlock the power of empathy and make our disconnected world a little more connected.

Your adventure in empathy starts now.

Chapter 1

What Is Empathy?

I remember a time when I sat across from an old friend at a coffee shop. We hadn't seen each other in years, and while I expected a joyful reunion, what unfolded was a monologue of woes from my friend. She was going through a tough divorce and needed someone to listen. As she poured her heart out, I found myself struggling to connect. I offered advice, tried to cheer her up, and even shared my experiences to make her feel less alone. Yet nothing seemed to help. Then it hit me: I wasn't genuinely listening or empathizing. I sympathized with and maybe even pitied her, but I didn't share her feelings or understand her pain. That day, I realized the profound difference empathy can make in our connections with others.

Definitions and Misconceptions About Empathy

DEFINITION: At its core, empathy is the ability to understand and share the feelings of another.

Empathy is about stepping into someone else's shoes and experiencing their emotions as if they were yours. This goes beyond just knowing what someone else feels; it's about feeling it, too. It's a shared experience that bridges the gap between two individuals, fostering a deeper connection. Unlike sympathy, which involves feeling sorry for someone, empathy immerses you in their emotional world, allowing you to connect more profoundly. Compassion takes empathy further by inspiring a desire to help alleviate the other person's suffering.

Empathy isn't a talent; it's a social skill you can build. Even if you lack empathy and are not a fan of heart-to-heart talks, you can learn to understand others better. Empathy isn't about getting emotional; it's about practical strategies for listening better, understanding others, and making interactions smoother. It's essential to balance empathy with objectivity for more effective communication.

One common misconception about empathy is that you must agree with the other person's viewpoint. This is far from the truth. Empathy is not about agreeing with someone's opinions or decisions. Instead, it's about understanding their perspective and acknowledging their emotions, even if you don't share the same views. This distinction is crucial, especially in today's world, where disagreements are frequent and often divisive. Empathy allows us to bridge these gaps without compromising our own beliefs.

Another misconception is that empathy is just about feeling sorry for someone. Feeling sorrow or pity distances you from the other person and suggests a sense of superiority, as if you're looking down on them from a higher place. Empathy, however, is about equality. It's about recognizing our shared humanity and the common emotions that unite us.

Many people also confuse empathy with emotional contagion. **Emotional contagion** is when you catch the emotions of others, like catching a cold. If someone is anxious, you become anxious; if they are joyful, you feel joyful. While related, empathy involves a conscious effort to understand and share another person's emotional state without losing your sense of self. It requires a balance between connecting with others and maintaining your emotional boundaries.

Historically, empathy has evolved from ancient philosophy to modern psychology. The ancient Greeks had the term "pathos," which referred to the emotional appeal in rhetoric. Fast forward to the 18th century, when the German philosopher Johann Gottfried Herder introduced the idea of "Einfühlung," or "feeling into," which laid the groundwork for our modern understanding of empathy. In the 20th century, psychologists like Carl Rogers and Daniel Goleman further expanded this concept, integrating it into theories of emotional intelligence and humanistic psychology.

Empathy is crucial in both personal and professional contexts.

- In our personal lives, it helps build meaningful relationships. When we empathize with our friends, family, or partners, we create spaces where they feel seen, heard, and valued. This deepens our connections and fosters trust.

- In the workplace, empathy enhances teamwork and collaboration. When leaders and team members understand and share each other's feelings, they create a supportive environment that boosts morale and productivity. Empathy also plays a crucial role in conflict resolution, allowing individuals to understand each other's perspectives and find common ground.

Culturally, empathy is viewed and practiced differently around the world.

- In Western cultures, empathy often manifests as a personal, individual experience. People are encouraged to express their emotions and connect on a one-on-one basis.

- In Eastern cultures, empathy is usually more communal. It's about understanding and prioritizing the collective well-being over individual emotions. Cultural practices such as communal gatherings and collective decision-making foster a sense of shared empathy.

- On a global scale, initiatives like empathy training programs and international humanitarian efforts aim to bridge cultural differences and promote a more empathetic world.

Empathy is not a one-size-fits-all concept. It varies across cultures, contexts, and individuals. However, its importance cannot be overstated. Empathy is the glue that holds us together in a disconnected world. It is a skill we can all develop and improve, and this book will provide you with the tools and techniques to do just that. You will learn how to enhance and apply your empathic abilities in your everyday life through practical exercises, real-life examples, and interactive elements.

DEFINITION: "Empathic" and "empathetic" both mean having the ability to understand and share the feelings of others. "Empathic" is the older term; "empathetic" is used more commonly in everyday language. Both terms are used in this book.

The Neuroscience of Empathy: How We Connect

Imagine sitting in a crowded subway, watching a young child drop their ice cream cone and burst into tears. As the child's face crumples, a pang of sadness hits you. You don't know this child, yet you feel a connection. This shared emotional experience is thanks to something fascinating happening in your brain: mirror neurons. These neurons activate when you perform an action and when you see someone else perform that same action. They allow you to "mirror" the emotions of others, making you feel their joy, pain, or frustration as if it were your own. This mirroring is a cornerstone of empathy, involving complex brain mechanisms that help us connect profoundly.

In neuroscience, empathy isn't just a vague feeling but a well-mapped process involving specific brain regions. The anterior insula and anterior cingulate cortex play pivotal roles in this intricate dance. The anterior insula helps you recognize and process feelings. In contrast, the anterior cingulate cortex is involved in emotional regulation and response. They enable you to understand and share another person's emotional state.

These brain regions communicate using neurotransmitters like oxytocin, often dubbed the "love hormone." Oxytocin fosters trust and social bonding, enhancing your ability to empathize. When you hug a friend or comfort a loved one, oxytocin levels rise, deepening your emotional connection.

Scientific studies have explored how empathy functions at the neurological level. Neuroscientific experiments using fMRI scans (functional magnetic resonance imaging) have shown that when you see someone in pain, the same brain regions light up as if you were experiencing the same pain yourself. This neural mirroring underscores the depth of human connection. For example, in a study where participants observed others experiencing physical discomfort, researchers noted significant activity in the anterior insula and anterior cingulate cortex—areas involved in emotional and pain processing. This suggests that our brains not only recognize but internally replicate feelings of distress, fostering empathy. The empathy-altruism hypothesis suggests that genuine empathy often leads to altruistic behavior, meaning that when you truly understand another's plight, you're more likely to help.

Two studies have shown that empathy has a genetic component, indicating that some of our empathic abilities are inherited. Yet, our environment and experiences also shape how empathetic we become.

Empathy isn't static; it develops and evolves throughout our lives. In childhood, empathy begins with what is perceived to be simple mimicry—infants cry when they hear other babies cry. As children grow, their cognitive skills improve, allowing them to see things from another's perspective. Parenting styles significantly influence this development. Children nurtured with empathy and understanding tend to develop more potent empathic abilities. As we move into adulthood, life experiences, cultural influences, and personal relationships further refine our empathic skills. Adolescence is particularly crucial, as this is when individuals learn to balance their emotions with others, a skill vital for healthy adult relationships.

Empathy is remarkably malleable; it can be enhanced or diminished over time. Practices like mindfulness and meditation have been shown to increase empathy. These techniques help you become more aware of your emotions, making it easier to connect with others.

On the flip side, trauma can negatively impact your ability to empathize. People who have experienced significant trauma can find it harder to relate to others due to the emotional scars they carry. However, empathy training programs offer them hope. These programs teach skills like active listening, perspective-taking, and emotional regulation, which can boost empathic abilities.

Understanding the neuroscience of empathy gives us a greater appreciation for this vital human trait. It's a soft skill with a complex interplay of brain functions that connects us to the world. Whether through the activation of mirror neurons or the influence of neurotransmitters like oxytocin, our brains are wired for empathy. This biological foundation underscores the importance of nurturing and developing our empathic abilities. Doing so can build stronger, more meaningful connections in our personal and professional lives.

Emotional Intelligence and Its Role in Empathy

Emotional Intelligence, or EI, has gained significant attention in recent years, and for good reason.

DEFINITION: At its core, **EI** is the ability to recognize, understand, and manage our own emotions while also being attuned to the feelings of others.

This dual focus makes EI powerful and relevant, especially in today's emotionally charged world. EI comprises four main components: self-awareness, self-management, social awareness, and relationship management.

- **Self-awareness** involves recognizing and understanding your emotions, which is the cornerstone of EI.
- **Self-management** takes this further by allowing you to control your emotional reactions and adapt to changing circumstances.
- **Social awareness**, which includes empathy, involves recognizing and

understanding the emotions of others.

- Finally, **relationship management** is about using this emotional understanding to navigate social complexities and build solid and healthy relationships.

Tools to measure EI, such as the Emotional Quotient Inventory (EQ-i) and the Mayer-Salovey-Caruso Emotional Intelligence Test (MSCEIT), offer valuable insights into how well we manage our emotional worlds.

Connecting EI to empathy might seem straightforward, but diving into the nuances is worth the effort. Social awareness, one of the four components of EI, directly includes empathy. When you are socially aware, you are in tune with the emotional currents around you, allowing you to respond appropriately. High EI enhances your empathic abilities by making you more perceptive to the subtle cues others give off, whether through body language, tone of voice, or facial expressions. This heightened perception allows you to connect deeper, building trust and understanding.

Moreover, empathy plays a crucial role in improving overall EI. When you empathize with someone, you engage in active listening and perspective-taking, critical aspects of relationship management. This cyclical relationship between EI and empathy means that as you improve one, the other naturally follows suit.

Benefits

The benefits of high emotional intelligence and empathy are manifold and touch nearly every aspect of life.

- In personal relationships, high EI allows you to navigate conflicts more effectively, understand your partner's, sibling's, child's, or parent's needs, and foster a deeper emotional connection.

- In the professional or higher educational realm, leaders with high EI are more adept at managing teams or classrooms, understanding employee or student motivations, and driving organizational or educational success. They can read the room, so to speak, and adjust their approach to meet their team's emotional needs.

- High EI also equips you with increased resilience and stress management skills. When you can understand and regulate your emotions, you are better prepared to handle life's ups and downs with grace and stability.

Developing EI is not passive; it requires active effort and practice.

- One effective tool for enhancing self-awareness is journaling. You gain insights into your emotional patterns and triggers by writing about your daily experiences and emotional reactions. This self-reflection helps you understand why you react the way you do and how to manage those reactions more effectively.

- Techniques for managing emotional reactions include deep breathing exercises, mindfulness practices, and cognitive reframing. These methods help you pause and consider your response before reacting impulsively.

- Role-playing scenarios are another excellent way to practice social awareness. Putting yourself in different social situations allows you to explore various responses and learn to read emotional cues more accurately.

EXERCISES:

1A. Reflection Prompt: Empathy and Emotional Intelligence

- Consider a recent interaction where emotions ran high—perhaps a difficult conversation with a colleague, a disagreement with a friend, or a stressful family situation.

- Reflect on your emotional response and the emotions displayed by others involved.

- Reflect on how empathy might have enhanced your emotional intelligence in this scenario. What could have been done differently to foster a better outcome?

- Repeat this reflection exercise using a recent interaction in a virtual meeting or over social media.

Incorporating these tools into your daily life can significantly enhance your EI and, by extension, your empathic abilities. Imagine a workplace where everyone practices high EI. Conflicts would be resolved more amicably, teamwork would flourish, and overall job satisfaction would skyrocket. Similarly, high EI fosters a better understanding and connection in personal relationships, making interactions more meaningful and fulfilling. The journey to developing high EI and empathy is ongoing, but the rewards are worth the effort, transforming your inner world and interactions with others.

Types of Empathy: Cognitive, Emotional, and Compassionate

DEFINITION: Cognitive empathy is understanding another person's perspective or mental state.

It's like putting on someone else's glasses to see the world through their eyes. This type of empathy involves understanding what others think and predicting their reactions. Still, it doesn't necessarily include sharing their feelings. Cognitive empathy is crucial in negotiation and conflict resolution, as it allows you to anticipate the needs and motivations of others. For example, consider a manager mediating a conflict between two employees. By understanding each employee's viewpoint and mental state, the manager can facilitate a more effective resolution, ensuring both parties feel heard and understood.

DEFINITION: Emotional empathy, on the other hand, is all about feeling what others feel.

Emotional resonance occurs when you share someone else's emotional experience. This type of empathy can be both good and bad. On the positive side, it enables deep connections and fosters intimacy in personal relationships. When a friend is grieving, emotional empathy allows you to share their sorrow, providing comfort and support. On the downside, emotional empathy can lead to burnout if you absorb too much of others' emotional pain without proper boundaries. This is why it's essential to balance emotional empathy with self-care practices.

DEFINITION: Compassionate empathy goes further by understanding and feeling another's emotions and taking action to help.

This type of empathy is often seen in caregiving and social work, where understanding and sharing the emotions of others isn't enough; there's a solid drive to alleviate suffering. For example, a nurse who feels a patient's distress and takes steps to provide comfort and care exemplifies compassionate empathy. This active component makes compassionate empathy a powerful tool for creating positive change and fostering a supportive environment.

While each type of empathy serves its purpose, they are interconnected and often overlap. Cognitive empathy helps you understand someone's situation, emotional empathy allows you to feel their pain, and compassionate empathy drives you to take action. Cognitive empathy might help you logically understand a colleague's frustration in a work setting. In contrast, emotional empathy lets you share their feelings, and compassionate empathy motivates you to offer support or solutions.

EXERCISES:

1B. Personal Connection

- Identify a personal relationship that could benefit from greater empathy.

- Write down three specific ways to show empathy in this relationship going forward.

- Repeat this exercise by identifying a virtual relationship, such as a remote coworker.

Balancing cognitive and emotional empathy is vital to a holistic understanding of others. Relying solely on cognitive empathy can make you seem detached, while excessive emotional empathy can overwhelm you. The synergy of combining all three types of empathy creates a comprehensive approach to connecting with others, whether in personal relationships, professional settings, or broader social contexts.

Empathy vs. Sympathy: Understanding the Difference

Sympathy and empathy are often used interchangeably, but they are distinct concepts that impact our relationships differently. Sympathy involves feeling pity or sorrow for someone else's misfortune. It creates an emotional distance, where you recognize the other person's suffering but remain somewhat detached. Sympathy often comes from a place of concern but lacks the deeper connection that empathy provides. When you're sympathetic, you might say, "I'm so sorry for your loss," offering a kind gesture but not necessarily sharing in the other person's emotional experience.

To illustrate the practical differences between empathy and sympathy, consider a scenario involving a friend who has just lost a loved one. Responding with sympathy might sound like, "I'm sorry for your loss. It's such a difficult time." This response, while well-meaning, can feel distant and impersonal, and if you're conversing in a virtual meeting or digitally, it's unlikely to promote a conversation. In contrast, an empathic response would involve sitting with your friend, listening to their stories about their loved one, and saying, "I can't imagine how hard this must be for you. I'm here with you." This approach fosters a more profound connection by acknowledging and sharing their grief. If meeting in person is impossible, try to meet virtually with cameras on and take more time to establish a friendly rapport.

The distinction between empathy and sympathy can also be significant in the workplace. Suppose a colleague is struggling with a heavy workload. A sympathetic response might be, "That sounds rough; I'm sorry you're so busy." While this shows concern, it doesn't offer much support. An empathic response, however, might be, "I can see you're under a lot of stress. Is there a part of your work that I can help you with?" This response acknowledges their struggle and offers practical support, strengthening your professional relationship.

Empathy fosters deeper connections by creating mutual understanding and support. When you empathize with someone, you validate their feelings and show that you genuinely care about their experiences. This mutual understanding builds trust and intimacy in personal and professional relationships. Sympathy, on the other hand, can unintentionally create a sense of hierarchy through pity.

Feeling sorry for someone can make them feel small or inferior, which might lead to resentment or a sense of isolation.

Practicing empathy over sympathy requires intentional effort and specific techniques. One effective method is active and reflective listening. **Active listening** involves focusing entirely on the speaker, avoiding interruptions, and showing that you're engaged through verbal and non-verbal cues. **Reflective listening** takes it further by paraphrasing what the speaker has said to ensure understanding, such as, "It sounds like you're feeling really overwhelmed right now."

Another approach to cultivating empathy is to validate others' feelings without offering unsolicited advice. Instead of jumping in with solutions, try to acknowledge their emotions first. Phrases like, "I can see why that would be frustrating," or "That must be really challenging for you," show that you understand and respect their feelings. This validation creates a safe space for them to express themselves more openly.

EXERCISES:

Exercises to enhance empathic responses in everyday interactions can also be beneficial.

1C. Practice empathy in low-stakes situations.

- Listen to a friend's minor complaint about their day.
- Focus on understanding their emotions and responding with empathy rather than advice.
- Try this over virtual and digital communication methods as well.

1D. Journal about your interactions with others

- Reflect on how you responded
- Identify opportunities to practice empathy in the future.

Understanding the difference between empathy and sympathy is crucial for building more profound, more meaningful connections. While both have their place, empathy offers a pathway to better understanding and support, fostering relationships built on trust and mutual respect. You can cultivate a more empathetic approach in all areas of your life by practicing active listening, validating others' feelings, and engaging in empathic exercises. This shift enhances personal and professional relationships and contributes to a more compassionate and connected world.

Summary Points

This chapter has laid the groundwork for understanding empathy and its importance. As we move forward, we'll review practical techniques and tools to further develop and apply empathy in various contexts, enriching our lives and relationships in profound ways.

CHAPTER 2

USE PRACTICAL TECHNIQUES FOR ATTENTIVE COMMUNICATION

Picture this: You're at a family dinner, and your cousin is sharing a story about a recent trip. You nod and mumble, "That's nice," while scrolling through your phone under the table. Your cousin's face falls, and the conversation fizzles. At the same time, another family member gives you a look of disapproval for your rude disengagement. Sound familiar? We've all been there, caught in the trance of our digital distractions, missing out on genuine human connection. This scenario underscores the importance of active listening, a foundational skill for effective empathic communication.

Active Listening: Techniques to Truly Hear Others

Active listening is more than just hearing words. It's about making a conscious effort to understand the complete message being communicated. When you actively listen, you focus entirely on the speaker, absorbing not just their words but their emotions, intent, and underlying messages. This listening depth is crucial for empathic communication, as it allows you to connect with others on a meaningful level. It involves putting aside external and internal distractions and giving full attention to the person speaking.

Fundamental techniques can significantly enhance your active listening skills.

- Maintaining eye contact, even in a virtual meeting, is a powerful way to show engagement. It signals to the speaker that they have your full attention, creating a sense of connection.

- Nodding and offering verbal affirmations like "I see" or "I understand" can further encourage the speaker, reassuring them that you are present and engaged.

- Avoiding interruptions is also vital. When you let someone speak without cutting them off, you show respect for their thoughts and feelings, creating a safe space for open communication.

However, active listening has its challenges.

- Internal distractions like personal biases and assumptions can cloud your listening ability. For example, if you're preoccupied with forming your response while the other person is speaking, you're not truly listening.

- External distractions, like noise or interruptions, can also hinder your focus.

These obstacles require conscious effort to overcome. Physically minimizing distractions can help, such as finding a quiet place to talk or turning off your phone. Additionally, adopting a mindset of curiosity and openness can help you set aside biases and assumptions, allowing you to fully engage with the speaker.

Consider engaging in specific exercises to practice and refine your active listening skills.

Exercises:

2A. Role-playing with a partner can be particularly effective.

- Take turns being the speaker and the listener. Focus on maintaining eye contact, offering verbal affirmations, and refraining from interruptions.
- After each round, provide feedback to each other on what worked, if any part sounded insincere, and what could be improved.
- Try this again with a partner in a virtual meeting.
- This exercise enhances your listening skills and fosters mutual understanding and respect.

2B. Keeping a listening log is another valuable exercise.

- At the end of each day, reflect on your listening experiences. Write down moments when you felt you listened well and when you struggled.
- What were the distractions or biases that got in the way? How did you handle them?
- This self-reflection can help you identify patterns and areas for improvement, making you more mindful of your listening habits.

Active listening is a skill that can transform communication and relationships. You can become a more empathetic and effective communicator by consciously listening to the complete message, avoiding distractions, and practicing fundamental techniques. This enhances your connections with others and fosters a more profound sense of understanding and mutual respect.

As you continue to practice and refine your active listening skills, you'll find that your conversations become deeper and more meaningful, creating a foundation for stronger, more empathic relationships.

Reflective Listening: Mirror Emotions for a Deeper Connection

Reflective listening is a technique that goes beyond merely hearing words. It involves mirroring the speaker's words to show you genuinely understand their message. This approach fosters a better connection by validating the speaker's emotions and experiences. When you reflectively listen, you become a mirror, reflecting the speaker's thoughts and feelings back to them. This validation makes the speaker feel heard and valued, which strengthens the emotional bond between the two of you. Reflective listening is not just about repeating words; it's about capturing the essence of what the speaker is saying and feeling and reflecting that back in a way that shows genuine understanding.

Paraphrasing is an effective technique for reflective listening. Paraphrasing involves restating the speaker's message in your own words to ensure clarity. For example, if a friend says, "I'm so overwhelmed with work right now," you might respond, "It sounds like you're feeling really stressed out at work." This shows that you're actively listening and trying to understand their situation.

Reflecting on another person's feelings is another effective technique. Try phrases like, "It sounds like you're feeling frustrated," or "You seem really excited about this." These phrases help to identify and validate the speaker's emotions.

Asking for confirmation is also essential. After reflecting on what you've heard, you might say, "Is that right?" This ensures that your interpretation is accurate and allows the speaker to affirm or clarify.

Benefits:

The impact of reflective listening on relationships can be profound.

- In personal relationships, reflective listening builds trust and rapport. When people feel heard and understood, they are more likely to open up and share their true feelings. This deepens the emotional connection and fosters mutual respect.

- In professional settings, reflective listening can reduce

misunderstandings and enhance collaboration. By validating colleagues' experiences and emotions, you create a supportive work environment where everyone feels valued. This improves team dynamics and boosts overall productivity and job satisfaction.

Let's look at some practical exercises to practice and improve your reflective listening skills.

Exercises:

2C. Paired exercises are particularly effective.

- Partner with a friend or family member and take turns sharing something on your mind, whether real or made up.
- As the listener, practice paraphrasing and reflecting feelings, then ask for confirmation.
- Provide feedback to each other on what worked well and what could be improved.
- Be sure to try this in a virtual meeting.

2D. Using reflective listening in conflict resolution scenarios is another excellent practice.

- When disagreements arise, paraphrase and confirm the other person's perspective and feelings before sharing your own.
- This approach can de-escalate tensions and lead to more constructive discussions.

2E. Journaling reflections on your experiences with reflective listening can also be beneficial.

- After engaging in a conversation, take a few minutes to write down what you did well and where you struggled.
- Reflect on how the other person responded and what you might do

differently next time.

- This self-reflection helps reinforce your learning and makes you more mindful of your listening strengths and weaknesses.

Reflective listening is a powerful tool for building deeper connections with others. By mirroring back what the speaker says and validating their emotions, you show that you genuinely understand and care about their experiences. This fosters trust, reduces misunderstandings, and enhances mutual respect in personal and professional relationships. Through practical exercises and self-reflection, you can develop and refine your reflective listening skills, making your interactions more meaningful and empathetic.

Non-Verbal Cues: Read Body Language and Facial Expressions

Imagine walking into a room where a meeting is underway. Before anyone speaks, you notice crossed arms, furrowed brows, and a mix of glaring and a lack of eye contact. Instantly, you sense tension and unease. The power of nonverbal communication encompasses body language, facial expressions, gestures, and posture. These silent signals speak louder than words, conveying emotions and intentions that words might mask or fail to express. Eye contact and physical proximity also play crucial roles, indicating interest, comfort, and engagement.

Reading non-verbal cues requires a keen awareness of consistency between verbal and non-verbal messages. For example, someone might say they are fine, but their slumped, closed, or turned-away posture and downcast eyes suggest otherwise.

Recognizing common facial expressions of emotions is another essential skill. Happiness often appears as a genuine smile with twinkling eyes. At the same time, sadness might show through a drooping mouth and lackluster gaze. Identifying body language that indicates openness or defensiveness is equally essential. Open arms and a forward-leaning posture suggest engagement, while crossed arms and averted eyes can indicate discomfort or resistance. Different participants in the same meeting might exhibit openness and defensiveness, depending on their role and level of engagement. It's important to observe all participants. In virtual meetings, all participants must turn their cameras on during discussions.

Non-verbal cues are invaluable in empathic communication. They enhance the accuracy of empathy by providing additional context to spoken words. When you observe non-verbal signals, you can better gauge someone's comfort and engagement levels. For example, noticing a colleague's clenched fists and rigid posture during a discussion about workload might prompt you to address their stress or frustration more thoughtfully. These cues allow you to respond more empathetically, fostering a deeper understanding and connection.

EXERCISES:

2F. Engage in non-verbal communication role-plays to practice reading non-verbal cues.

- Partner up and take turns expressing different emotions without speaking. Focus on conveying feelings through facial expressions, gestures, and posture.

- After each round, discuss what emotions were communicated and how accurately they were interpreted.

- Try this exercise in a virtual meeting with cameras on, and notice when non-verbal communication isn't detectable.

- This exercise sharpens your ability to read and respond to non-verbal signals effectively.

2G. Another exercise involves watching silent videos.

- Watch a scene from a movie or a TV show with the sound off and try to interpret the characters' emotions based solely on their body language and facial expressions. Pay attention to their eye movements, gestures, and posture.

- Afterward, watch the scene with sound to see how well your interpretations matched the dialogue.

- This practice helps you hone your skills in reading non-verbal cues in real time.

2H. Keeping a journal of observed non-verbal cues in daily interactions can also be enlightening.

- Throughout your day, note the nonverbal signals you observe in others and how they align with or contradict their spoken words.

- Reflect on how these cues influenced your understanding of the situation and responses.

- This ongoing reflection deepens your awareness of non-verbal communication and its impact on your interactions.

Non-verbal cues are a rich source of information in any interaction. By paying close attention to body language, facial expressions, and other non-verbal signals, you can better understand others' emotions and intentions. This enhances your empathic abilities and improves your overall communication skills. In personal relationships, professional settings, or casual encounters, mastering the art of reading non-verbal cues can transform how you connect with others.

Empathic Questioning: Ask the Right Questions to Understand

Empathic questioning is a powerful communication tool designed to show genuine interest and understanding. It involves asking questions, encouraging deeper conversation, and allowing the speaker to open up and share more about their thoughts and feelings. This approach is not just about gathering information; it's about creating a space where the speaker feels valued and understood. By asking the right questions, you can uncover the emotions and intentions behind the words, fostering a deeper connection.

Use open-ended questions to enhance your questioning skills. These questions cannot be answered with a simple "yes" or "no." Instead, they invite the speaker to elaborate and share more. For example, you might ask, "How did that make you feel?" or "Can you tell me more about that?" These questions signal that you are genuinely interested in their experience and encourage them to share their thoughts and emotions more freely. It's equally important to avoid leading or judgmental questions, which can make the speaker feel defensive or judged. Instead, aim for neutral and open questions, allowing the speaker to express themselves without feeling pressured.

Follow-up questions are another essential technique in empathic questioning. Once the speaker has shared their initial thoughts, use follow-up questions to delve deeper into their feelings and experiences. For example, if someone mentions being stressed about work, you might ask, "What specifically is causing you the most stress?" or "How does this stress affect your day-to-day life?" These questions show that you actively listen and engage with their experience. They also help the speaker to explore their feelings more thoroughly, leading to greater self-awareness and insight.

With empathic questioning, you encourage the speaker to share more, making them feel heard and understood. This builds trust and rapport, strengthening the connection between you. Thoughtful inquiry demonstrates that you value their perspective, which fosters mutual respect and openness.

- In professional settings, empathic questioning can facilitate team collaboration and problem-solving by encouraging candid and meaningful discussions.

- In personal relationships, it deepens emotional bonds and promotes understanding.

EXERCISES:

2I. Engage in questioning with a partner to practice and refine your empathic questioning skills.

- Take turns being the speaker and the listener, focusing on asking open-ended and follow-up questions.

- After each round, provide feedback on what worked well and what could be improved.

2J. Reflecting on your conversations is another valuable exercise.

- After a significant conversation, take a few minutes to think about the questions you asked. Were they effective in encouraging the speaker to share more? Did they help you understand their feelings and experiences better?

- Identify any questions that came across as judgmental or leading, and think about how you might rephrase them next time.

2K. Create a list of go-to empathic questions for various scenarios.

- Consider different contexts in which you might need to use empathic questioning, such as a work meeting, a casual conversation with a friend, or a conflict resolution scenario.

- Write down a few open-ended and follow-up questions for each context. For example, in a work meeting, you might use questions like, "What are your thoughts on this project?" or "How do you feel about the proposed changes?"
In a personal conversation, you might ask, "What has been the most challenging part of this experience for you?" or "How can I support you right now?"

- This list can be a handy reference, helping you quickly recall practical questions when needed.

Empathic questioning is a skill that can transform your communication and relationships. By asking questions that show genuine interest and understanding, you encourage deeper conversation and foster a sense of connection and trust. In professional settings or personal relationships, asking the right questions can enhance empathy and understanding, making your interactions more meaningful and impactful.

Practice Empathy in Digital Communication: Emails, Chats, and Social Media

Digital communication presents unique challenges to practicing empathy. One of the biggest hurdles is the lack of non-verbal cues and immediate feedback. In face-to-face interactions, we rely heavily on body language, facial expressions, and tone of voice to gauge emotions and intentions. These cues are absent in text-based communication, making it harder to understand the full context of a message. This absence can lead to misunderstandings and misinterpretations, as the emotional nuances often get lost in translation. An email intended to be friendly might come off as curt, or a joke in a chat might be taken the wrong way, leading to unnecessary conflicts.

Use clear and considerate language to enhance empathy in digital communication.

- Take the time to craft thoughtful responses, considering how your words might be perceived by the recipient.

- Avoid using ambiguous phrases or sarcasm that could be misinterpreted, opting for straightforward and kind language.

- Pay attention to the tone and emotional content of your messages.

- Emojis and punctuation can help convey emotions that words alone might not fully capture. For example, a simple smiley face at the end of a sentence can indicate friendliness and soften the tone.

Practicing empathy online is crucial in our digital age. Building and maintaining relationships despite physical distance is more important than ever. Empathy can help reduce conflicts and foster positive connections, whether it's in professional settings or personal interactions. When you take the time to understand and respond to the emotions behind the words, you create a more supportive and understanding environment. This approach strengthens relationships and promotes a healthier and more respectful online community.

Let's look at specific exercises to improve your empathic skills in digital communication.

Exercises:

2L. Reflect on past digital conversations.

- Take a moment to review your recent emails, chats, or social media interactions.
- Identify instances where misunderstandings occurred and consider how they could have been handled differently.
- Were there moments where more straightforward language or a more considerate tone could have made a difference?
- Was there an attempt at humor or sarcasm which fell flat?
- This reflection can help you become more mindful of your communication habits and identify areas for improvement.

2M. Practice empathic responses in online role-playing scenarios.

- Partner up with a friend or colleague and simulate different online interactions.
- Take turns being the sender and the receiver of messages, focusing on crafting thoughtful and empathetic responses.
- After each round, provide feedback to each other on what worked well, what assumptions were made by the reader of the text, and what could be improved.

- This practice can help you develop a more nuanced understanding of how to communicate empathy in digital formats.

2N. Keeping a journal of digital interactions and self-reflections can also be beneficial.

- Throughout your day, make a habit of jotting down notes about your online communications.

- Reflect on your feelings during these interactions and how others might have perceived your messages. Consider what you did well and where you could improve.

- This ongoing reflection helps reinforce your learning and makes you more conscious of your communication style.

Summary Points

Incorporating these techniques and exercises into your daily routine can significantly enhance your empathy in digital communication. You can build stronger, more empathetic connections online by using clear and considerate language, crafting thoughtful responses, and paying attention to your messages' tone and emotional content. This improves your personal and professional relationships and contributes to a more compassionate and understanding digital community. As we navigate this increasingly digital world, the ability to communicate with empathy will become an invaluable skill, helping us bridge the emotional gaps that technology often creates.

CHAPTER 3

RECOGNIZE DIVERSE PERSPECTIVES

I remember a heated argument with a coworker about a new project. We were both so entrenched in our viewpoints that we couldn't see eye to eye. It wasn't until I took a step back and tried to see the situation from his perspective that I realized he had valid concerns. This shift in mindset not only resolved our disagreement but also strengthened our working relationship. My experience underscored the importance of perspective-taking, a crucial skill that allows us to walk in someone else's shoes and see the world through their eyes.

Walk in Someone Else's Shoes: Techniques for Perspective-Taking

Perspective-taking is understanding another person's viewpoint, thoughts, and feelings. It's about stepping outside your experiences and considering how someone else perceives a situation. This skill is essential for developing empathy because it helps you connect with others more deeply. When you can see the world from another person's perspective, you can better understand their emotions and motivations. This understanding fosters mutual respect and improves communication, making it easier to build meaningful relationships.

Exercises:

3A. Imagine yourself in the other person's situation to take their perspective. This mental exercise involves placing yourself in their shoes and considering how you would feel and react.

- For example, if a friend is upset about a breakup, try to recall a time when you experienced a similar loss. How did it feel? What thoughts went through your mind? This exercise helps you connect with their emotions and better understand their experience.

- Additionally, ask yourself how the other person might feel or think, which can provide valuable insights. Consider their background, experiences, and current circumstances. What might be influencing their perspective?

- This reflective questioning can help you see beyond your own biases and assumptions.

3B. Role-playing exercises are another powerful tool for enhancing perspective-taking skills.

- Partner with a friend or family member and take turns playing different roles in various scenarios. For example, one person could play the role of a frustrated customer, while the other could play the role of a service representative.

- After each role-play, discuss what it felt like to be in each role and what insights you gained.

- Repeat this exercise using a virtual meeting.

- This practice improves your understanding of different perspectives and enhances your empathy and communication skills.

Benefits

The benefits of perspective-taking extend beyond individual relationships.

- Perspective-taking fosters a more inclusive and respectful environment by reducing biases and prejudices. When you understand where someone else is coming from, you are less likely to judge them based on stereotypes or preconceived notions.

- This mutual understanding promotes harmony and reduces conflicts in personal and professional settings.

- Additionally, perspective-taking enhances your problem-solving abilities by allowing you to consider multiple viewpoints.

- This comprehensive approach leads to more innovative and effective solutions, as it considers all stakeholders' diverse needs and perspectives.

Exercises:

3C. Engage in reflective journaling to practice perspective-taking. This exercise involves writing about your experiences from another person's perspective.

- For example, if you disagree with a colleague, write a journal entry from their point of view.

- How did they perceive the situation?

- What emotions and thoughts might they have experienced?

- This practice helps you develop empathy and understand others' perspectives.

3D. Engage in discussions or debates where you must argue from an opposing viewpoint. This challenges you to step outside your comfort zone and consider different perspectives, enhancing your ability to empathize.

3E. Watch films or read books that offer diverse perspectives to enrich your perspective-taking skills. Choose stories that depict experiences different from yours, and reflect on how the characters' backgrounds and circumstances shape their viewpoints. This exposure to diverse narratives broadens your understanding of the world and deepens your empathy.

Perspective-taking is a transformative skill that enhances empathy, improves relationships, and fosters a more inclusive and understanding environment. By imagining yourself in another person's situation, asking reflective questions, and engaging in role-playing exercises, you can develop this crucial skill and enrich your connections with others. Through reflective journaling, discussions, and exposure to diverse narratives, you can continue to expand your perspective-taking abilities and become a more empathetic and understanding individual.

Cultural Sensitivity: Recognize and Respect Differences

I remember attending a workshop on cultural sensitivity a few years ago. The facilitator began with a simple yet powerful exercise: we were asked to share a story from our childhood that shaped who we are today. As people from different backgrounds narrated their experiences, it became evident how diverse our lives were. Yet, there was a common thread of humanity that connected us all. This exercise highlighted the need for cultural sensitivity, which is the awareness and respect for cultural differences. Suppose you understand that everyone's background shapes their worldview. In that case, this can prevent **ethnocentrism**, a perspective where you view your culture as superior, leading to unfair judgments.

Actively learn about different cultures and traditions to enhance your cultural sensitivity. This includes understanding their customs, values, and social norms. Start by reading books or watching documentaries about various cultures.

Even better, engage in conversations with people from different backgrounds. Ask them about their traditions, holidays, and cultural practices. This broadens your knowledge and shows respect and genuine interest in their way of life. Practicing active listening and open-mindedness is crucial in these interactions. Instead of listening to respond, focus on understanding their perspective. This means setting aside your judgments and being open to new ideas and viewpoints.

Avoid stereotypes and assumptions for cultural sensitivity. Stereotypes are oversimplified ideas about a group of people, often based on limited information. They can be harmful and lead to misunderstandings. For example, assuming that everyone from a particular country shares the same traits ignores each person's individuality. Instead, approach each interaction with curiosity and a willingness to learn. Recognize that everyone's experiences are unique and shaped by many factors.

Cultural sensitivity significantly enhances empathic abilities.

- When you understand and respect cultural differences, you build stronger cross-cultural relationships. This understanding fosters trust and mutual respect, making connecting on a deeper level easier. It also enhances communication and reduces misunderstandings.

- When you are aware of cultural nuances, you can adjust your communication style to be more effective and respectful, leading to more meaningful and productive interactions.

- Additionally, cultural sensitivity fosters inclusivity and diversity. By valuing different perspectives, you create a more welcoming and supportive environment for everyone.

To visualize this concept, consider a Venn diagram like the one shown here, in which each of the three circles represents a unique culture with its own nuances.

- Where the circles overlap, the intersected area represents where the cultures share things in common.

- Communication between people of different cultures (i.e., different circles), which reflects what they have in common (i.e., where the circles overlap), is clearly understood.

- Communication that includes cultural uniqueness(i.e., not from or to the intersecting circles that represent things in common)is likely to be misunderstood.

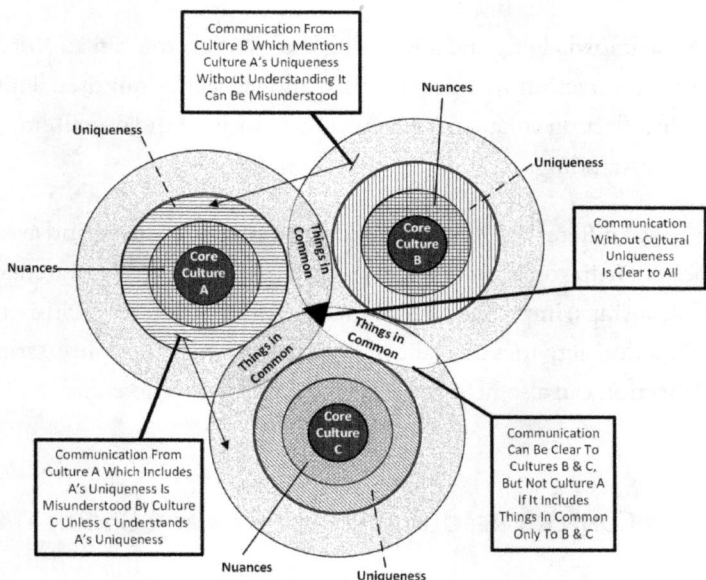

Communication With Other Cultures Requires Awareness and Sensitivity

EXERCISES:

3F. Participate in cultural exchange programs or events to develop cultural sensitivity. These programs provide firsthand experiences of different cultures, allowing you to immerse yourself in their customs and traditions. Whether it's a local cultural festival or an international exchange program, these experiences broaden your understanding and appreciation of diversity.

3G. Engage in conversations with individuals from diverse backgrounds by seeking opportunities to interact with people from different cultures, whether it's through community events, social groups, or online platforms. Listen to their stories, ask questions, and share your own experiences.

3H. Reflect on your cultural biases and how they affect your interactions. Consider how your background and experiences shape your views.

- Do you hold any biases or assumptions?

- How might these impact your interactions with others?

- By acknowledging and addressing these biases, you can approach each interaction with a more open and respectful mindset. This self-reflection enhances your cultural sensitivity and overall empathy and understanding.

Learning about different cultures, practicing open-mindedness, and avoiding stereotypes can help you become more culturally sensitive. This awareness fosters robust relationships, improves communication, and promotes inclusivity and diversity. Practical activities like cultural exchanges, engaging conversations, and self-reflection can also help you continually develop and enhance cultural sensitivity.

EMPATHY IN CONFLICT RESOLUTION: FIND COMMON GROUND

Conflicts are inevitable. Whether it's a misunderstanding with a friend, a disagreement with a colleague, or a family argument, conflicts arise from differing perspectives and unmet needs. Empathy is crucial in conflict resolution because it helps us understand both parties' underlying emotions and needs. When you empathize with someone during a conflict, you create a safe space for open communication. This space allows both sides to express their feelings and concerns without fear of judgment or retaliation. Understanding these emotions and needs is the first step toward finding common ground and resolving the conflict effectively.

- **Active listening** is the first step in empathic conflict resolution. It means focusing entirely on the other person, avoiding interruptions, and showing engagement through nodding or verbal affirmations. Active listening helps you understand both perspectives, which is crucial for resolving conflicts.

- **Reflective listening** goes a step further by validating the other person's emotions. When you mirror their feelings and acknowledge their experiences, you make them feel heard and respected. For example, if someone complains, "No one is helping me with this project," you might respond with, "It sounds like you want more participation on the project by other team members." This simple act of validation can defuse tension and pave the way for more constructive dialogue.

- **Active de-escalation techniques** are vital in managing the emotional intensity during a conflict. Techniques such as maintaining a calm tone, using non-threatening body language, and choosing words that are non-provocative can significantly reduce the heat of an argument. For example, during a heated discussion, consciously lowering your voice can encourage the other person to do the same, which may make the environment less confrontational.

- **Asking open-ended questions** is another powerful technique in empathic conflict resolution. These questions encourage the other person to share their feelings and issues more. Instead of asking, "Are you upset?" which prompts a yes or no answer, try asking, "Can you tell me more about what's bothering you?" This approach helps uncover more profound issues that might take time to be apparent. It also shows that you are genuinely interested in understanding their perspective, which can build trust and mutual respect. By exploring these deeper issues, you can identify the root cause of the conflict and work toward a solution that addresses both parties' needs.

- Adding to these strategies, **using "I-statements"** can help prevent the other person from becoming defensive. This technique involves speaking about your feelings and needs without blaming the other person. For example, instead of saying, "You never listen to me," you could say, "I feel unheard when I talk about my ideas, and I need to know that my input is valued." This way, you express your feelings and needs without making the other person feel accused, facilitating a more empathetic dialogue.

Benefits

Using empathy in conflict resolution has several benefits.

- First, it builds trust and mutual respect. When people feel understood and validated, they are more likely to reciprocate and approach the conflict with an open mind. This mutual respect makes finding common ground and reaching a resolution easier.

- Second, empathy reduces tension and hostility. Acknowledging and validating the other person's emotions can defuse anger and frustration, making the conversation more productive.

- Finally, empathic conflict resolution leads to more effective and lasting solutions. When both parties feel heard and respected, they are more likely to agree on a solution that meets everyone's needs.

This collaborative approach fosters a sense of ownership and commitment to the resolution.

Exercises:

3I. To develop your conflict resolution skills, consider engaging in role-playing scenarios.

- Partner up with a friend or colleague and simulate different conflict situations.

- Focus on practicing active and reflective listening, asking open-ended questions, and validating emotions.

- After each role-play, discuss what worked well and where there is room for improvement.

- Repeat this exercise via a virtual meeting, and see what challenges that adds.

- This practice helps you become more comfortable using empathy in real-life conflicts.

3J. Reflecting on past conflicts can also be enlightening.

- Think about a recent disagreement you had. How did you handle it? Were there opportunities where empathy could have made a difference?

- Write down your reflections and identify specific moments where you could have listened more actively, validated the other person's emotions, or asked open-ended questions.

- This self-reflection helps you learn from past experiences and apply these lessons in future conflicts.

3K. Practicing mediation techniques that emphasize empathy is another valuable exercise.

- Mediation involves facilitating a conversation between two parties in conflict, helping them understand each other's perspectives and work toward a resolution.

- As a mediator, you create a safe space for open communication, practice active and reflective listening, and ask open-ended questions to explore deeper issues.

- This practice enhances your conflict resolution skills and deepens your empathy and understanding of different perspectives.

BUILD EMPATHY THROUGH STORYTELLING: SHARE PERSONAL NARRATIVES

There's something magical about stories. Think about the last time you were deeply moved by a story, whether a book, a movie, or even a friend's personal tale.

- Stories have the power to create emotional connections through shared experiences. When people share their personal narratives, they invite others into their world, making understanding and feeling their emotions easier.

- This is why storytelling is such a powerful tool for building empathy. By sharing your stories and listening to others, you tap into a well of understanding and compassion that might otherwise remain untouched.

Compelling storytelling requires a couple of key techniques.

- Use vivid and relatable details. Paint a picture with your words that allow others to see, hear, and feel what you experienced. For example, instead of saying, "I was sad," describe the scene: "The rain poured down as I sat on the porch, feeling the weight of the world pressing on my shoulders." This kind of detail brings your story to life and makes it more engaging.

- Expressing genuine emotions and experiences is also crucial. Don't be afraid to show vulnerability. Sharing your true feelings, whether joy, fear, or sorrow, helps others connect with you on a deeper level. It's this honesty that fosters empathy.

Listening to others' stories without judgment is equally essential.

- When someone shares their narrative, give them your full attention. Avoid interrupting or offering unsolicited advice. Instead, focus on understanding their experience and emotions.

This active listening shows respect and empathy, making the storyteller feel valued and heard. It's in these moments of genuine connection that empathy flourishes.

Storytelling breaks down barriers and stereotypes. When you hear someone's personal narrative, you see them as individuals rather than stereotypes. Their story humanizes them, making it harder to hold onto prejudices. This is especially powerful in diverse communities where people from different backgrounds can share their experiences and find common ground.

Storytelling also fosters a sense of community and belonging. People share their stories and create a collective narrative that binds them together. This shared understanding strengthens relationships and builds a supportive network.

Moreover, storytelling encourages self-reflection and personal growth. When sharing your stories, you gain insights into your experiences and emotions.

This self-reflection helps you understand yourself better and fosters individual growth. Listening to others' stories can also prompt you to reflect on your life and consider new perspectives. This reciprocal process of sharing and reflecting deepens empathy and enriches your emotional world.

EXERCISES:

3L. To practice storytelling, start by writing and sharing personal narratives in a group setting.

- Find a supportive group where members take turns sharing their stories. This could be a book club, a community group, or even an informal gathering of friends.

- As you share your narrative, focus on using vivid details and expressing genuine emotions.

- Encourage others to do the same.

- This practice enhances your storytelling skills and builds a stronger sense of community.

3M. Listening to and reflecting on others' stories is another valuable exercise.

- When someone shares their narrative, listen actively and without judgment.

- Afterward, take a moment to reflect on what you learned from their story. How did it make you feel? What insights did you gain?

- Writing these reflections in a journal can deepen your understanding and empathy.

3N. Participating in storytelling workshops or events can also be incredibly enriching. These settings provide a structured environment for practicing and honing your storytelling skills. You can share your stories, receive feedback, and listen to diverse narratives. This immersive experience can significantly enhance your empathy and storytelling abilities.

Storytelling is a powerful tool for building empathy. Sharing personal narratives and listening to others creates emotional connections that foster understanding and compassion. Using vivid details, expressing genuine emotions, and actively listening without judgment make storytelling effective. Through this practice, you break down barriers, foster community, and encourage personal growth.

Empathy in Diverse Work Environments: Create Inclusive Spaces

I'll never forget my first time working in a truly diverse team. We came from different countries, spoke various languages, and had unique life experiences. Yet, what united us was a shared commitment to our project and a mutual respect fostered by empathy.

This environment illustrated to me how empathy is crucial for creating inclusive workplaces. It fosters a culture of respect and understanding where everyone feels valued and heard. Empathy enhances collaboration and teamwork in a diverse work environment, enabling people from different backgrounds to work harmoniously.

Creating an empathic workplace starts with encouraging open and honest communication. This means creating an atmosphere where employees feel safe to express their thoughts, concerns, and ideas without fear of judgment.

- Holding regular team meetings where everyone has the opportunity to speak can help. These meetings should be structured to ensure quieter voices are heard and all opinions are valued.

- Another practical method is providing diversity and inclusion training. Such training programs educate employees about different cultures, biases, and stereotypes, helping them understand and appreciate their colleagues' diverse backgrounds. This education builds a foundation of respect and empathy, which is essential for an inclusive work environment.

Opportunities for team-building and relationship-building are also vital.

- Organize activities that require collaboration, such as team-building exercises or group projects, to strengthen bonds among team members. These activities should be inclusive and considerate of everyone's abilities and preferences. For example, a team-building exercise could involve solving a complex problem, encouraging communication, cooperation, and mutual support.

- Social events like team lunches or after-work gatherings can provide informal settings for employees to get to know each other better, fostering deeper connections and understanding.

Benefits

The benefits of an empathic workplace are manifold.

- First and foremost, it improves employee satisfaction and retention. Employees who feel understood and valued are more likely to be engaged and committed to their work. This sense of belonging reduces turnover and fosters loyalty.

- An empathic workplace also enhances creativity and innovation. When people from diverse backgrounds feel comfortable sharing their ideas, they bring many perspectives that can lead to innovative solutions and approaches.

- Furthermore, empathy reduces workplace conflicts and misunderstandings. Employees can constructively navigate disagreements by understanding and respecting each other's viewpoints, leading to a more harmonious work environment.

Exercises:

To develop and apply empathic skills at work, consider conducting team-building exercises that emphasize empathy and collaboration.

30. One effective exercise is the "empathy circle."

- Have team members take turns sharing their experiences and feelings while others listen without interrupting.

- This practice fosters a deeper understanding of each other's perspectives and promotes mutual respect.

3P. Encouraging regular feedback and open dialogue is another valuable practice.

- Create channels for employees to share their thoughts and concerns, whether through anonymous surveys, suggestion boxes, or open-door policies.

- This feedback loop ensures that everyone's voice is heard and valued, fostering a culture of continuous improvement and empathy.

Reflecting on workplace interactions and identifying opportunities for empathy is also crucial.

3Q. After a meeting or a challenging conversation, take a moment to reflect on how you handled the interaction.

- Did you actively listen and validate the other person's feelings? Were there moments where you could have shown more empathy?

- Write down your reflections and think about how you can apply these insights in future interactions.

- This ongoing self-reflection helps you become more mindful of your empathic behavior and continuously improve your skills.

Empathy is the cornerstone of a diverse and inclusive work environment. By fostering open communication, providing education on diversity, and creating opportunities for team-building, you can cultivate a workplace where everyone feels valued and respected. This environment can improve employee satisfaction and retention, enhance creativity, and reduce conflicts. With self-reflection, you can apply empathic skills to transform your workplace into a supportive and inclusive space for all.

Summary Points

Empathy is indispensable for creating inclusive workplaces. It fosters respect, enhances collaboration, and builds a positive work environment. By incorporating empathy into daily interactions and workplace culture, you contribute to a more harmonious and productive space. This foundation leads us into the next chapter, where we will explore self-empathy and self-care techniques to further enrich our personal and professional lives.

CHAPTER 4

FOCUS ON SELF-EMPATHY AND SELF-CARE TECHNIQUES

I magine this: You've had a long, exhausting day. Your boss was demanding, your commute was a nightmare, and you're ready to collapse. You finally get home, but instead of relaxing, you start beating yourself up for not handling things better. You replay every mistake, every awkward moment, and every missed opportunity, feeling worse with each passing minute.

This harsh self-criticism is all too common, and many struggle with it. But what if I told you there's a way to treat yourself with the same kindness and understanding you offer others? That's where self-empathy comes in.

Recognize Why Self-Empathy Is Essential

Self-empathy is the practice of recognizing and validating one's own emotions. It's about understanding and accepting personal feelings without judgment. When you practice self-empathy, you acknowledge your emotions—joy, sorrow, anger, or fear—and fully allow yourself to feel them. This acknowledgment helps you understand your emotional state and provides a foundation for emotional well-being.

Unlike self-pity, which involves feeling sorry for yourself, or self-indulgence, which can lead to avoiding responsibilities, self-empathy is about balance. It's about treating yourself with the same compassion and respect you would offer a friend in a similar situation.

The significance of self-empathy lies in its ability to foster self-acceptance and self-compassion.

- When you practice self-empathy, you create a space to be honest about your feelings and experiences. This honesty leads to greater self-acceptance as you learn to embrace all parts of yourself, including the less-than-perfect ones.

- Self-compassion, which involves treating yourself with kindness during suffering or failure, naturally follows. When self-compassionate, you offer comfort and understanding, reducing the harsh self-criticism that often accompanies difficult emotions.

According to Harvard Health, practicing self-compassion can significantly improve both mental and physical health, reducing anxiety and depression, and fostering a sense of inner peace.

Benefits

The benefits of self-empathy are far-reaching.

- By reducing self-criticism, self-empathy enhances self-esteem, helping you feel more confident and secure in yourself.

- It also improves emotional regulation by allowing you to process and manage your emotions more effectively.

- When you understand and validate your feelings, you are better equipped to navigate emotional challenges with resilience and stability.

- This resilience fosters healthier relationships as you become more attuned to your needs and better able to communicate them to others.

- Understanding your emotions also makes it easier to empathize with others, as you recognize similar feelings and experiences.

Exercises:

4A. To cultivate self-empathy, start with self-reflection exercises. Take a few minutes each day to check in with yourself.

- Ask yourself how you're feeling and why.

- Write down your thoughts and emotions without judgment.

- This practice helps you recognize and validate your feelings, making understanding and accepting them easier.

4B. Journaling is another powerful tool for exploring your emotions. Use these prompts to guide your writing:

- "What emotions did I experience today?"

- "What triggered these emotions?"

- Reflecting on your emotional experiences through journaling can provide valuable insights and foster greater self-awareness.

Compassionate self-talk is also essential for practicing self-empathy. When you catch yourself engaging in negative self-talk, pause and reframe your thoughts with kindness.

- Instead of saying, "I'm such a failure," try saying, "I'm doing the best I can, and it's okay to make mistakes."

This shift in perspective can significantly change how you feel about yourself. Treat yourself with the same kindness you would offer a friend. If a friend were struggling, you wouldn't berate them or dismiss their feelings. Extend that same compassion to yourself.

However, practicing self-empathy can be challenging. Societal pressures and cultural norms often discourage self-compassion, promoting the idea that self-criticism is necessary for success. Overcoming these pressures requires a conscious effort to challenge and reframe these beliefs. Recognize that self-compassion is not a sign of weakness but a source of strength.

- Develop a supportive inner dialogue. Pay attention to how you talk to yourself and try to be kind and understanding. When you notice self-critical thoughts, counter them with compassionate ones.

Internalized self-criticism is another common barrier to self-empathy. Many of us have an inner critic constantly pointing out our flaws and mistakes. Recognizing and challenging this inner critic is essential for practicing self-empathy.

- When you notice your inner critic spewing self-critical thoughts, ask yourself if you would say the same thing to a friend. If not, reframe the thought with compassion. Instead of thinking, "I'm so bad at this," reframe it as, "I'm still learning, and it's okay to make mistakes."

By practicing self-empathy, you can foster a healthier relationship with yourself. Recognizing and validating your emotions, engaging in compassionate self-talk, and challenging self-critical thoughts are powerful ways to cultivate self-empathy. These practices improve your mental health and well-being and enhance your ability to connect with others on a deeper level. So, take a moment to show yourself the kindness and compassion you deserve. You are worthy of empathy from both others and yourself.

Daily Self-Care Practices for Empaths

DEFINITION: Being an **empath** means you have an extraordinary ability to deeply feel and absorb the emotions of others. It's like having a finely tuned emotional radar, constantly picking up on the feelings of those around you.

This heightened sensitivity can be both a gift and a challenge. On one hand, it allows you to connect with others profoundly, offering comfort and understanding in ways few can. On the other hand, it can leave you feeling overwhelmed and emotionally drained, especially if you don't take time to care for yourself. That's why daily self-care is not just a luxury for empaths; it's a necessity.

Regular self-care is vital for maintaining emotional balance. Without it, the emotional weight of others' feelings can lead to burnout and overwhelm. When you're constantly absorbing the emotions of those around you, it's easy to lose sight of your needs and boundaries. Self-care acts as a buffer, allowing you to recharge and reconnect with yourself. It enhances your overall well-being and quality of life, allowing you to navigate your empathic abilities with grace and resilience.

Many self-care practices can help you maintain emotional balance.

- Mindfulness meditation is one such practice. You can center and calm your mind by taking a few minutes each day to sit quietly and focus on your breath. This practice helps you distinguish your own emotions from those you've absorbed from others, bringing clarity and peace.

- Physical activities like yoga, walking, or dancing are also excellent for stress relief. These activities get your body moving and help release pent-up emotions and tensions.

- Engaging in creative outlets such as painting, writing, or playing music can also be therapeutic. These activities allow you to express your emotions safely and constructively, providing an outlet for your feelings and fostering a sense of accomplishment and joy.

Benefits

Routine self-care practices offer numerous benefits for empaths.

- Establishing a regular self-care routine creates a sense of stability and predictability in your life. This stability can be grounding, providing a solid foundation to navigate daily life's emotional ups and downs.

- Regular self-care also improves emotional regulation and resilience. When you take time each day to care for yourself, you become better equipped to handle emotional challenges with grace and stability.

- Furthermore, self-care enhances self-awareness and self-understanding. Regularly checking in with yourself and attending to your needs, you gain a deeper understanding of your emotions and what you need to thrive.

Action Items

Integrating self-care into your daily life doesn't have to be complicated.

- Start by setting aside dedicated time for self-care activities. This could be as simple as scheduling 10 minutes each morning for mindfulness meditation or setting aside an hour each evening for a relaxing bath or a walk in nature.

- Creating a self-care toolkit can also be helpful. Fill this toolkit with your favorite self-care activities and resources, such as a journal, essential oils, a list of affirmations, or a favorite book. These readily available tools make it easier to practice self-care, even on busy days.

- Look for small moments throughout the day to practice self-care. This could be taking a few deep breaths before a meeting, stepping outside for a few minutes of fresh air, or writing a quick gratitude note in your journal.

These small acts of self-care add up, helping you maintain emotional balance and resilience.

Incorporating these self-care practices into your daily life can significantly affect how you manage your empathic abilities. Taking time each day to care for yourself creates a solid foundation of emotional health and well-being. This foundation allows you to navigate the world with empathy and compassion without losing sight of your needs and boundaries. So, take a moment to prioritize yourself and make self-care an integral part of your daily routine. You deserve it.

Regulate Your Emotions: Techniques to Manage Emotional Overload

Emotional regulation is crucial for empaths. It's the ability to manage intense emotions without being overwhelmed. For empaths, emotions can often feel like tidal waves, crashing and pulling in every direction. Emotional regulation helps you navigate these waters, providing the tools to stay afloat rather than being swept away. It enhances emotional resilience, allowing you to maintain stability even when emotions run high. This stability is essential for managing empathic sensitivity's emotional highs and lows.

- **Deep breathing exercises** are incredibly effective at calming the nervous system. When you feel overwhelmed, take a moment to pause and focus on your breath. Inhale deeply through your nose, hold for a few seconds, and then exhale slowly through your mouth. This simple act can signal your body to relax, reducing stress and anxiety.

- **Progressive muscle relaxation** is another powerful technique. It involves tensing and slowly releasing each muscle group, starting from your toes and working your way up to your head. This practice helps release physical tension, which often accompanies emotional stress.

- **Visualization techniques** are also beneficial for creating a sense of calm and safety. Imagine a place where you feel completely at ease, whether it's a beach, a forest, or a cozy room. Close your eyes and visualize this place in as much detail as possible. Engage all your senses—imagine the sounds, smells, and textures. This mental escape can provide a respite from overwhelming emotions, grounding you in peace and security.

Benefits

Effective emotional regulation has a profound impact on overall well-being.

- By managing your emotions, you can significantly reduce stress and anxiety, leading to a calmer and more balanced life.

- Emotional regulation also enhances resilience, making it easier to bounce back from emotional challenges. This adaptability is crucial for navigating life's ups and downs.

- Additionally, better emotional management improves relationships. When you can regulate your emotions, you are less likely to react impulsively or lash out, fostering healthier and more constructive interactions.

Action Items

Practicing emotional regulation requires consistent effort and practice.

- Start with **guided meditations** focused on emotional balance. These meditations often include deep breathing, visualization, and mindfulness, helping you develop the skills to manage your emotions effectively.

- Another helpful exercise is **journaling** about emotional triggers and responses. Take time each day to reflect on what triggered your emotions and how you responded. Writing down your thoughts can provide valuable insights into your emotional patterns, helping you identify areas for improvement.

- **Mindfulness** in daily activities is another excellent way to stay present and centered. Whether eating, walking, or washing dishes, focus entirely on the task. Pay attention to the sensations, sights, and sounds around you. This practice helps you stay grounded in the present moment, making it easier to manage your emotions as they arise.

EXERCISES:

4C. Guided Meditation for Emotional Balance

- Find a quiet place where you won't be disturbed.

- Sit comfortably and close your eyes. Take a few deep breaths to center yourself.

- Imagine a warm light surrounding you, bringing peace and safety.

- As you breathe in, visualize this light filling your body, calming your mind, and soothing your emotions.

- As you exhale, imagine releasing any tension or stress.

- Continue this process for a few minutes, allowing the light to envelop you completely.

- When you're ready, slowly open your eyes and take a moment to notice how you feel.

Emotional regulation is a skill that takes time to develop, but the benefits are well worth the effort. By incorporating techniques like deep breathing, progressive muscle relaxation, and visualization into your daily routine, you can manage your emotions more effectively and improve your overall well-being. Mindfulness and reflecting on your emotional triggers can provide valuable insights, helping you navigate your empathic sensitivity with greater ease and stability.

Stay Present and Connected with Grounding Techniques

Imagine feeling like you're floating away, detached from the here and now, overwhelmed by a flood of emotions. Grounding techniques are like an anchor that keeps you tethered to the present moment, helping you stay connected and centered.

Grounding techniques are vital for empaths, who often absorb the emotions of those around them. They help reduce feelings of dissociation and overwhelm, allowing you to remain present and engaged. Grounding is about reconnecting with your body and the physical world, providing stability and calm amid emotional turbulence.

Sensory grounding focuses on physical sensations like touch, taste, and smell.

- You might start by holding a piece of ice, feeling its coldness and how it melts in your hand. You could savor a piece of chocolate, paying attention to its texture and flavor. These simple acts can pull you back to the present moment, anchoring you in the here and now.

- Another method is to use essential oils or scented candles to engage your sense of smell. The familiar and comforting scents can help soothe your mind and bring you back to calm.

Mental grounding engages your mind with activities that require focus and concentration.

- This can be as simple as counting backward from 100 or listing all the countries you can think of. These mental tasks distract your mind from overwhelming emotions and help you regain control.

- Another technique is to describe your surroundings in detail. Look around and note the colors, shapes, and textures of the objects around you. This exercise grounds you and enhances your awareness of the present moment.

Physical grounding involves connecting with your body through movement or touch.

- This can be achieved by taking a short walk and focusing on the sensation of your feet hitting the ground with each step.

- Alternatively, you might engage in a brief exercise routine or stretch, paying attention to how your muscles feel as they move.

- Even placing your hands under running water and focusing on the temperature and sensation can help ground you.

These physical activities help you reconnect with your body, providing a sense of stability and presence.

Benefits

The benefits of grounding techniques are manifold.

- By reducing anxiety and panic, grounding helps you maintain emotional stability and well-being.

- When you're grounded, you can think more clearly and make better decisions, enhancing your focus and mental clarity. This clarity is essential for empaths, who often feel overwhelmed by absorbing others' emotions.

- Grounding techniques also improve emotional regulation and resilience. By staying connected to the present moment, you can better manage your emotions and healthily respond to stress.

Exercises:

Consider incorporating specific exercises into your daily routine to develop your grounding skills.

4D. Sensory walks are a great way to engage your senses while enjoying the benefits of nature.

- As you walk, focus on the sights, sounds, and smells around you.

- Notice the colors of the leaves, birds chirping, and the scent of flowers or fresh grass.

- This practice grounds you and enhances your appreciation of the natural world.

4E. Grounding meditations are another powerful tool. These guided practices focus on bringing awareness to the present moment, often through deep breathing and visualization.

- Imagine roots growing from your feet into the earth, anchoring you firmly in place. This visualization can provide a profound sense of stability and connection.

4F. Using **grounding objects** can also be helpful during stressful moments.

- Keep a small, tactile object with you, such as a smooth stone or a piece of fabric.
- When you feel overwhelmed, hold the object and focus on its texture, weight, and temperature.
- This simple act can bring you back to the present moment, providing comfort and security.

Grounding techniques offer a practical and effective way to stay present and connected, especially for empaths who often feel overwhelmed by their sensitivity. Incorporating sensory, mental, and physical grounding practices into your daily life can enhance your emotional stability and well-being. These techniques provide valuable tools for managing stress and maintaining balance through sensory walks, meditations, or using grounding objects.

Build Emotional Resilience: Practices to Strengthen Your Inner Self

DEFINITION: Emotional resilience is the capacity to bounce back from emotional challenges and stress.

Emotional resilience is crucial for empaths, who often feel emotions intensely. It's the ability to navigate life's ups and downs without being overwhelmed. Building emotional resilience enhances overall mental health and well-being. It allows you to handle stress more effectively, maintain emotional stability, and find footing even when life throws curveballs. When you're resilient, you can face adversity with a sense of hope and strength rather than feeling defeated.

Gratitude practices can help develop a positive mindset; they are one of the most effective ways to build emotional resilience. Take a few moments each day to reflect on what you're grateful for, to shift your focus from what's going wrong to what's going right. This simple practice can lift your mood and foster a sense of contentment.

Building **strong social connections** is equally important. A support network of friends and loved ones provides a safety net of encouragement and understanding. These connections can offer comfort during tough times and celebrate your victories, big or small.

Engaging in **regular physical activity** is another powerful tool. Exercise boosts your mood by releasing endorphins, increases energy levels, and helps you feel more grounded and in control.

BENEFITS

The benefits of emotional resilience extend far beyond just feeling good.

- By reducing the impact of stress and adversity, resilience helps you maintain a sense of balance and well-being.

- It enhances emotional stability, making adapting to changes and challenges easier without losing equilibrium.

- This adaptability fosters a sense of empowerment and self-efficacy as you begin to trust your ability to handle whatever comes your way.

- When you're emotionally resilient, you're not just surviving but thriving. You have the confidence to take on new challenges, pursue your goals, and build a fulfilling life.

EXERCISES:

4G. To practice building emotional resilience, start with daily gratitude journaling.

- Each day, write down three things you're grateful for. They can be as simple as a sunny day, a kind word from a friend, or a delicious meal.

- This practice trains your mind to focus on the positive aspects of your life, fostering a more optimistic outlook.

4H. Positive affirmations are another powerful tool.

- Each morning, look in the mirror and repeat affirmations that reinforce your self-belief, such as "I am strong," "I can handle this," or "I am worthy of love and happiness."

- These affirmations can boost your confidence and resilience, especially when faced with challenges.

Engaging in activities that challenge and build resilience is also essential. This might involve learning a new skill, taking on a new project at work, or facing a fear. These activities push you out of your comfort zone and help you build confidence in your abilities. Each time you overcome a challenge, you strengthen your resilience, proving you can handle adversity. Moreover, these experiences provide valuable lessons and insights, helping you grow and develop.

Emotional resilience is not something you're born with; it's a skill you can develop with practice. By incorporating gratitude practices, building strong social connections, engaging in regular physical activity, and challenging yourself with new experiences, you can strengthen your inner self and enhance your ability to bounce back from emotional challenges. This resilience improves your quality of life and empowers you to face the future with confidence and hope.

Summary Points

You can improve your mental health and connect better with others by practicing self-empathy, validating your emotions, engaging in compassionate self-talk, and challenging self-critical thoughts. Developing emotional regulation is worth the effort. Grounding techniques help you stay present and connected, which helps you manage stress. Emotional resilience is enhanced by practicing gratitude and building connections. These foundations of self-empathy and self-compassion will serve you well as we explore more advanced techniques for applying empathy in various aspects of your life in the following chapters.

Publisher's Note

For more on Self-Empathy, see Delia Sike's companion book, Overthinking—The Silent Saboteur.

CHAPTER 5

SET HEALTHY BOUNDARIES

Picture this: you're at a family gathering, and your aunt asks you to help her move some furniture this weekend. You've had a grueling week at work and only want to relax. Yet, the word "no" gets stuck in your throat, and you find yourself agreeing, even though it's the last thing you want to do. You feel a knot of resentment forming in your stomach, knowing you've overcommitted once again. This scenario is all too common and underscores the importance of setting healthy boundaries.

DEFINITION: Boundaries are clear limits a person sets to protect their emotional well-being, energy, and time while maintaining healthy relationships. They help ensure that empathetic individuals can offer care and support without being overwhelmed, manipulated, or drained by the needs or demands of others.

In the context of empathy, boundaries allow people to be kind and helpful while safeguarding their own mental and emotional health by distinguishing between supporting others and overextending themselves.

Recognize the Need for Boundaries: Signs and Symptoms

What are the signs and symptoms that a leader needs to establish boundaries?

- **Chronic feelings of being overwhelmed and burnt out** are some of the first signs that you need better boundaries. When you constantly feel drained after interactions, it's a red flag. This emotional exhaustion often stems from taking on too much responsibility and not allowing yourself the space to recharge. Over time, this leads to burnout, where you feel mentally and physically depleted, unable to muster the energy for even simple tasks.

- **Growing resentment** toward others for overstepping their bounds is another sign. You might feel irritated or angry when someone asks for a favor, even if it's something minor. This resentment often arises because you feel taken advantage of or unappreciated. It signals that your boundaries have been repeatedly violated and you've reached your limit.

- Physical symptoms like **fatigue and stress-related ailments** are also indicators. When your body is constantly stressed due to overcommitment, it can manifest in various ways, such as headaches, muscle tension, or digestive issues. These physical symptoms are your body's way of telling you that something needs to change.

Difficulty saying "no" is a common struggle. You might find yourself agreeing to tasks or favors to satisfy others. This often leads to overcommitting, where you take on more than you can handle. The inability to say "no" stems from a desire to be liked or a fear of conflict. Still, it ultimately results in stress and resentment.

Impacts

The impact of poor boundaries on relationships can be profound.

- Strained relationships due to unmet expectations are common.

- When you consistently prioritize others' needs over your own, you set a precedent that can be difficult to break.

- People may begin to expect that you will always say "yes," leading to imbalanced relationships where your needs are overlooked. This dynamic can cause feelings of being taken advantage of or unappreciated, further straining the relationship.

- Increased conflicts and misunderstandings often follow as unmet needs and unspoken frustrations surface.

Examples

Consider specific scenarios that illustrate boundary violations.

- A friend who frequently borrows money without repayment can create a sense of exploitation. You might feel obligated to help but resentful when they don't follow up.

- A colleague who regularly interrupts your personal time with work demands can blur the lines between professional and personal life, leading to stress and frustration.

- Family members making unreasonable emotional demands, such as expecting you to be their constant emotional support, can leave you drained and unappreciated.

EXERCISES:

5A. Recognizing the need for boundaries starts with self-reflection. Journaling about recent interactions and feelings of discomfort can provide valuable insights.

- Write down instances where you felt overwhelmed or resentful.
- Reflect on these situations to identify patterns. Were there specific people or contexts that triggered these feelings?

5B. Reflecting on past situations where your limits were overstepped can also be enlightening.

- Think back to times when you felt taken advantage of or unappreciated.
- What were the circumstances?
- How did you respond, and how did it affect you?

5C. Identifying patterns of behavior that lead to emotional exhaustion is crucial.

- Are there recurring themes in your interactions?
- Do you notice that you often say "yes" when you want to say "no"?
- Understanding these patterns helps you pinpoint where boundaries are needed.

This self-awareness is the first step toward setting and maintaining healthy boundaries. It allows you to recognize the signs early and proactively protect your well-being.

By paying attention to these signs and reflecting on your experiences, you can begin to understand where boundaries are lacking and take steps to establish them. This enhances your well-being and improves relationships by fostering mutual respect and understanding.

Practical Steps to Set Boundaries: Scripts and Scenarios

Setting clear and firm boundaries is not just about saying "no" but protecting your well-being and emotional health. Boundaries are essential for establishing mutual respect in relationships with family, friends, or colleagues. When you set boundaries, you communicate your limits and needs, clarifying what you will and won't tolerate. This helps prevent resentment and ensures that your relationships remain balanced and healthy.

Exercises:

5D. To start setting boundaries, you must clearly define your personal limits and needs, which involves some introspection.

- Think about what makes you uncomfortable or stressed. It could be constant interruptions during downtime or being asked to take on extra work when you're already swamped.

- Write these down to help you understand where your boundaries need to be.

5E. Once you've identified your limits, the next step is communicating them assertively and respectfully.

- Use clear, direct language without being aggressive. It's about standing your ground while respecting the other person's feelings.

Consistency is vital when enforcing boundaries. You need to stand firm even when you face pushback. People might not like your boundaries, especially if they're used to you always saying "yes." But it's crucial to reinforce the message that your boundaries are non-negotiable. This consistency builds trust and respect. When others see that you're serious about your limits, they're more likely to respect them. It also helps avoid confusion and mixed signals. If you waiver on your boundaries, it can send a message that they're flexible, leading to further boundary violations.

EXERCISES:

5F. Scripts can be beneficial when setting boundaries, especially if you find it challenging to find the right words when needed. Here are a few examples.

- If you need some personal time, you might say, "I need some time alone to recharge this weekend." This clearly communicates your need for space without being confrontational.

- If someone brings up a topic you're uncomfortable discussing, you can say, "I'm not comfortable discussing this topic right now." This clearly limits the conversation while respecting the other person's perspective.

- If you're asked to take on more than you can handle at work, you might say, "I can't take on any additional work at the moment." This communicates your limit without leaving room for negotiation.

BENEFITS

- Maintaining consistency in boundary-setting reinforces the message that your boundaries are serious. It's like building a muscle—the more you practice, the stronger and more natural it becomes. Imagine telling a friend you can't lend them money anymore. The first few times they ask again, it might be tough to say no, but it becomes easier each time you reinforce that boundary. Over time, your friend will understand and respect that limit.

- Consistency also builds trust and respect. When people know where you stand, it creates a sense of reliability. They know what to expect from you, which fosters mutual respect. This is especially important in professional settings. Consistently enforcing your workplace boundaries sets a standard for how you expect to be treated, enhancing your credibility and professional relationships.

- Another reason consistency is essential is to avoid confusion and mixed signals. If you're inconsistent with your boundaries, it sends a message that they're negotiable. This can lead to further boundary violations and increased frustration. For example, suppose you sometimes answer work emails after hours, but other times you don't. In that case, it can create confusion about your availability. By consistently sticking to your boundaries, you clarify what is acceptable and what isn't, reducing the chances of misunderstandings.

By defining your limits, communicating assertively, and maintaining consistency, you can set effective boundaries that protect your well-being and foster healthier relationships. Use scripts to help navigate tricky conversations, and remember that consistency is vital to reinforce your boundaries.

Maintain Boundaries Without Guilt: Emotional Independence

Imagine standing in your kitchen, phone in hand, as a friend on the other end asks for another favor. You've already helped them move last weekend, lent them money, and listened to hours of their troubles. Your instinct is to say yes, but exhaustion hits you. This is where emotional independence comes into play.

DEFINITION: Emotional independence means relying on yourself for emotional validation and support rather than seeking it from others.

Emotional independence is about reducing dependence on others' approval and acceptance, allowing you to set boundaries without the crippling fear of disappointing someone.

Many people struggle to overcome guilt when setting boundaries. One practical method is to reframe guilt as a sign of growth and self-care.

- When you feel guilty for saying no, remember it's a healthy step toward caring for your needs.

This perspective shift can make setting boundaries feel less like selfishness and more like an investment in your well-being. It's similar to the discomfort you feel when exercising to get back in shape; you know it will pass.

Practicing self-compassion and self-forgiveness is also crucial.

- Give yourself permission to prioritize your needs without feeling bad about it.

- Acknowledge that it's okay to put yourself first sometimes.

- Remind yourself of the benefits of healthy boundaries: they protect your energy, reduce stress, and improve your overall quality of life.

Societal and cultural expectations can heavily influence our feelings of guilt. Many societies place a high value on selflessness and sacrifice, particularly for women. These norms can make it difficult to set boundaries without feeling like you're letting others down. Cultural expectations often prioritize others' needs over personal well-being, reinforcing that taking care of oneself is selfish.

EXERCISES:

5G. To challenge and overcome these societal and cultural pressures, start by questioning these societal norms.

- Ask yourself if these expectations truly serve you or hold you back from living a balanced and fulfilling life.

- Surround yourself with supportive people who understand and respect your need for boundaries.

- It's also helpful to seek role models who embody healthy boundary-setting behaviors.

Developing emotional independence requires intentional practice.

5H. Journaling about your personal values and priorities can be a powerful exercise.

- Take time each day to write about what matters most and how you can align your actions with these values.

- This practice helps you stay grounded and focused on what's truly important, making it easier to set and maintain boundaries.

5I. Practicing mindfulness is another effective way to build emotional independence.

- Engage in mindfulness exercises that keep you present and connected to yourself.
- Whether through meditation, deep breathing, or simply walking in nature, mindfulness helps you tune into your needs and emotions.

5J. Setting small, manageable boundaries can build confidence over time.

- Start with something simple, like setting aside 30 minutes daily for yourself, free from interruptions.
- As you become more comfortable with these smaller boundaries, gradually take on bigger ones.
- This incremental approach helps you develop the skills and confidence to set and maintain boundaries without feeling overwhelmed. It also allows you to experience the positive impacts of boundaries in gradual, manageable steps.

Emotional independence empowers you to set boundaries without guilt. You can navigate societal pressures and prioritize your well-being by relying on yourself for emotional validation, reframing guilt, and practicing self-compassion. Journaling, mindfulness, and setting small boundaries can build the confidence and skills needed to maintain these limits efficiently. Prioritizing your needs is not an act of selfishness; it's a necessary step toward a healthier, more balanced life.

Handle Pushback: Dealing with Resistance to Your Boundaries

When you start setting boundaries, you might face pushback. Pushback is resistance from others who are accustomed to the lack of boundaries. Imagine this: you've always been the go-to person for last-minute favors at work. One day, you decide to set a boundary and decline a request. Your colleague reacts with surprise, maybe even frustration. They might try to guilt-trip you, saying things like, "You've always helped me before," or use manipulation tactics to get you to change your mind. These emotional reactions, whether anger, guilt-tripping, or subtle manipulation, are common forms of pushback.

Effectively handling pushback requires a blend of calmness and assertiveness.

- Staying calm is crucial. When you remain composed, you defuse the situation's emotional charge. Take deep breaths and remind yourself of your right to set boundaries.

- Assertiveness comes next. Use clear and firm language to reaffirm your boundaries without engaging in arguments. You might say, "I understand this is important to you, but I've already made other plans." This statement acknowledges their perspective while reinforcing your boundary. Using "I" statements to express personal needs and feelings can also help. For example, "I feel overwhelmed when I take on too many tasks, so I need to focus on my current workload."

Facing resistance can be emotionally draining, making self-care vital during these times.

- Seek support from trusted friends or a therapist who can offer encouragement and perspective. Talking through the situation with someone who understands can provide emotional relief and reinforce your resolve.

Practicing self-compassion and self-validation is also crucial.

- Remind yourself that setting boundaries is a form of self-care and that it's okay to prioritize your needs.

- Engage in stress-relief activities like exercise or meditation to help manage the emotional toll of pushback. Whether it's a brisk walk, a yoga session, or a few minutes of deep breathing, these activities can help you stay grounded and focused.

EXERCISES:

Building confidence in dealing with resistance takes practice.

5K. Role-playing scenarios with a friend or partner can be incredibly helpful.

- Take turns being the person setting the boundary and the one pushing back.

- Try this role-playing in a virtual one-on-one meeting, to see if it's easier or harder.

- This exercise allows you to practice your responses and get comfortable with the language you need to use.

5L. Reflecting on past experiences of pushback and identifying what worked can also offer valuable insights.

- Think about a time when you successfully maintained a boundary.

- What strategies did you use?

- How did you feel afterward?

- Reflecting on these experiences reinforces your ability to handle pushback effectively.

5M. Creating a list of affirmations to reinforce personal boundaries can be a powerful tool.

- Write statements reminding you of your right to set boundaries and their benefits. For example, "I have the right to prioritize my needs," or "Setting boundaries helps me maintain my well-being."

- Keep this list handy and refer to it whenever you face resistance.

- These affirmations act as a mental anchor, helping you stay firm and confident in your decision.

Experiencing pushback is a natural part of setting boundaries, especially if others are used to you always saying "yes." You can navigate resistance effectively by staying calm and assertive, using "I" statements, and seeking support. Practicing self-care, role-playing scenarios, and reflecting on past successes further bolsters your confidence. Affirmations remind you of your right to set boundaries, reinforcing your resolve in the face of pushback.

Boundaries in Professional Settings: Navigate Workplace Dynamics

Setting boundaries in the workplace is crucial for maintaining professional success and well-being. Without clear boundaries, you risk burnout, unfair competition, and a disrupted work-life balance. Constantly working late hours or checking emails during family dinners is a sign that boundaries are blurred. This can lead to chronic stress and exhaustion, making it hard to recharge and perform effectively. Maintaining clear boundaries helps preserve your energy, ensuring you're at your best at work and home.

Boundaries also enhance productivity and job satisfaction. Setting realistic expectations for your workload and deadlines allows you to focus on tasks without feeling overwhelmed. This clarity will enable you to prioritize effectively, leading to higher-quality work and more significant accomplishments.

Additionally, boundaries build professional respect and credibility. When you communicate your limits assertively and consistently, colleagues and supervisors are more likely to respect your time and contributions. This mutual respect fosters a positive work environment where everyone's needs are acknowledged and valued.

- One of the first steps in setting boundaries with colleagues and supervisors is clearly communicating your availability and limits. For example, to avoid being contacted after hours, make this known by setting an automatic email response stating your office hours. This simple step can go a long way in managing expectations.

- Another technique is to set realistic expectations for your workload and deadlines. Be honest about what you can reasonably accomplish within a given timeframe. If a project's scope expands beyond your capacity, communicate this early to avoid overcommitment.

Action Items

Workplace boundary challenges are common and can test your resolve. Addressing boundary violations assertively and professionally is also essential.

- If colleagues repeatedly **interrupt your personal time** with work demands, address them directly. You might say, "I understand this project is important, but I must balance work and personal time. Can we discuss this during office hours?" This approach acknowledges the task's importance while reaffirming your boundaries.

- Handling **after-hours work requests** is a frequent issue. When faced with such requests, it's essential to assess the urgency. If it's not a real emergency, reiterate your availability and suggest addressing it the next business day.

- Managing **personal relationships with colleagues** can also blur boundaries. While it's natural to form friendships at work, it's vital to maintain professional limits. For example, avoid discussing sensitive personal issues during work hours to keep the focus on professional tasks.

- Dealing with **micromanagement** or overbearing supervisors is another challenge. In such cases, it's crucial to communicate your need for autonomy. You might say, "I appreciate your guidance, but I work best when I have some autonomy to manage my tasks. Can we agree on regular check-ins to update you on my progress?" This approach shows respect for their role while asserting your need for space.

Exercises:

To practice setting workplace boundaries, engage in assertive communication exercises.

5N. Role-playing scenarios with a colleague or friend can be particularly effective.

- Take turns practicing boundary-setting conversations, focusing on clear and assertive language.
- Repeat this role-playing in a virtual one-on-one meeting, and note any added complications.
- After each role-play, provide feedback to each other on what worked and what could be improved.

5O. Reflecting on past workplace interactions can also offer valuable insights.

- Think about times when your boundaries were respected and when they were not.
- What strategies did you use, and what might you do differently next time?
- Write these reflections in a journal to help solidify your learning and make you more mindful of your boundary-setting habits.

5P. Creating a personal boundary plan for professional settings can also be beneficial.

- Outline your critical boundaries, such as availability, workload limits, and how you'll handle boundary violations.
- A written plan provides a clear reference point and helps you stay consistent in your boundary-setting efforts. It can also remind you of your commitment to maintaining a healthy work-life balance.

Summary Points

Setting boundaries in the workplace is vital for preventing burnout, enhancing productivity, and building respect. You can navigate workplace dynamics effectively by communicating availability, setting realistic expectations, and addressing violations professionally. Practicing assertive communication, reflecting on past interactions, and creating a personal boundary plan will help you maintain these boundaries consistently.

As we move forward, let's explore how empathy plays a role in leadership, balancing compassion with objectivity to create a supportive and effective work environment.

* Help Us Spread Empathy *

"Kindness is a language which
the deaf can hear and the blind can see."

Mark Twain

Did you know that performing acts of kindness can boost your happiness and even your health? We believe that spreading empathy can change the world, and we're excited to have you on this journey with us.

Here's something to ponder: Would you lend a helping hand to someone you've never met, even if you were not recognized for it? Think about this person for a moment. They might be someone eager to improve themselves, someone who seeks connection and understanding but doesn't know where to start.

Our goal is to make empathy a universal language. We aim to reach as many hearts and minds as possible, and we need your help to do it.

Your voice is powerful. Many people decide which books to read based on recommendations like yours. That's why I'm asking you to leave a review for **Empathy Unlocked – Learning to Connect in a Disconnected World**.

Leaving a review is a small, simple act that takes less than a minute but can profoundly impact someone's life.

Your thoughts can help:
- one more person understand their family better.
- one more leader create a compassionate workplace.
- one more individual navigate relationships with kindness.
- one more community become a little closer, a little warmer.
- one more story of connection begin.

Ready to share some kindness? It's easy! Just go to this book on Goodreads or on the website for the company from which you purchased the book, and leave your review with a rating, a video or photo, and your thoughts.

If this book has touched you, consider passing it on to someone else who might benefit from it.

With heartfelt thanks,
Delia Sikes

Chapter 6

Lead with Empathy

I magine a leader who listens to your concerns and genuinely seeks to understand them. This type of leader stands out in a world where corporate environments often feel cold and transactional. I recall a time when I worked for a manager who embodied empathy. During a particularly stressful project, he noticed the strain on our team. He called for a meeting—not to discuss deadlines but to check in on us as individuals. He asked us how we were coping and offered support. This simple act of empathy transformed our work environment, making us feel valued and understood.

If you think empathy is just a 'soft' skill that won't help your career, think again. Empathic communication is the secret behind top leaders' success. Empathy can boost collaboration, reduce conflict, and advance your career, whether you're leading a team or navigating office dynamics.

The Empathic Leader: Characteristics and Benefits

An empathic leader possesses several key traits that set them apart.

- Active listening skills and open communication are at the forefront. Such leaders don't just hear words; they listen to the emotions and intentions behind them.

- They create an environment where team members feel safe expressing their ideas and concerns. This open communication fosters trust and transparency, essential for a healthy workplace.

- These leaders also show a genuine concern for their employees' well-being. They understand that their team members are not just cogs in a machine but individuals with unique needs and aspirations. This genuine care builds a foundation of mutual respect and loyalty.

Empathic leaders excel in understanding and managing emotions, both their own and those of their team members. They recognize when someone is stressed or upset and take proactive steps to address these emotions. This emotional intelligence allows them to navigate complex interpersonal dynamics effectively. Furthermore, they are committed to creating a supportive work environment. They prioritize work-life balance and ensure their team has the resources and support needed to thrive. This commitment goes beyond mere words; it reflects their daily actions and decisions.

Benefits

The benefits of empathic leadership are substantial and far-reaching.

- **Open and honest communication** becomes the norm, creating a transparent and trusting environment. This trust extends beyond individual relationships, building mutual respect among all team members.

- **Increased employee engagement and job satisfaction** are among the most notable benefits. When employees feel understood and valued, their sense of belonging and inclusivity makes everyone feel like they are part of a cohesive team. They are more likely to be committed to their work.

- **Higher productivity and better performance** are likely outcomes of increased engagement as employees adopt more efficient team processes.

- **Team collaboration and innovation** are enhanced. Empathic leaders foster an inclusive and supportive environment, encouraging their teams to share ideas and work together effectively. This collaborative spirit leads to innovative solutions and a more dynamic workplace.

- **Improved conflict resolution and workplace harmony** are also positive outcomes of empathic leadership. By addressing emotions and fostering open communication, these leaders can resolve conflicts more effectively and maintain a harmonious work environment.

- **Additional benefits include reduced turnover and absenteeism**. Employees who feel supported and appreciated are less likely to leave their positions or take unnecessary sick days.

- **Reduced recruitment and training costs** benefit the organization due to this stability.

Empathic leadership behaviors include these specific actions.

- Regular one-on-one check-ins with team members show the leader values each individual's well-being and professional growth.

- Offering flexible work arrangements to accommodate personal needs demonstrates a commitment to work-life balance.

- Recognizing and celebrating employees' achievements reinforces a culture of appreciation and motivation.

- Providing constructive and supportive feedback helps employees grow and improve without feeling criticized or demoralized.

Exercises:

6A. Reflection Exercise: Empathic Leadership Self-Assessment
Take a moment to reflect on your leadership style. Consider the following questions and jot down your thoughts:

- How often do you check in with your team member s on a personal level?

- Do you give equal time to remote team members via virtual meetings? Do you travel to meet with them in-person periodically?

- Do you actively listen to your team's concerns, or do you find yourself formulating responses while they speak?

- Do you support and defend your team in the presence of your leaders and peers? Do you seek buy-in for the improvements they have suggested? Do you get answers to their questions that you didn't already know?

- How do you accommodate the personal needs of your team members, such as flexible work arrangements?

- How do you recognize and celebrate your team's achievements?

- When providing feedback, do you focus on support and growth, or do you tend to criticize?

- Use these questions to identify areas where you excel as an empathic leader and areas where you need to improve.

By consciously practicing empathic leadership behaviors, you can create a more supportive, innovative, and harmonious work environment for your team.

Build a Culture of Empathy: Strategies for Organizational Change

Imagine entering an office where everyone greets each other warmly, collaboration is the norm, and employees genuinely care about one another. This is what it means to have an empathic organizational culture. In this space, empathy is prioritized in every aspect, from policies to daily practices.

This kind of environment doesn't happen by accident; it requires intentional actions and commitment from leadership. Prioritizing empathy means ensuring it is a core value embedded in the organization's mission and everyday operations. Policies and practices should reflect this commitment, creating a consistent and supportive atmosphere.

Action Items

Establish empathy training and workshops to foster empathy at the organizational level.

- These sessions can educate employees about the importance of empathy, teach practical skills, and provide practice opportunities.

- Workshops should include activities like role-playing scenarios where participants practice empathic responses or group discussions to explore the impact of empathy on the workplace.

- Provide resources and support for ongoing empathy development to ensure employees have the tools and encouragement to continue growing their empathy skills.

- These experiences build empathy skills and reinforce the organization's commitment to creating a supportive environment.

Establish mentorship programs that emphasize empathy; this can also make a significant difference.

- Pair new employees with experienced mentors who model empathic behaviors to help integrate empathy into the company's culture from day one.
- Mentors can provide guidance, support, and a safe space for new hires to express their concerns and ideas.
- This mentorship fosters a culture of continuous learning and support, where empathy is passed down through generations of employees.

Encourage collaborative and team-building activities to further strengthen an empathic culture.

- Activities that require teamwork and open communication help build trust and understanding among team members.
- Whether it's a group project, a team-building retreat, or even casual social events, these activities create opportunities for employees to connect personally.
- This connection fosters empathy, making it easier for team members to support one another and work together effectively.

Implement work-life balance policies to support the whole employee; this is crucial.

- Policies that allow for flexible work hours, remote work options, and sufficient leave for personal and family needs show employees that their well-being is a priority.
- Employees who feel supported in balancing work and personal lives are more likely to be engaged and productive.
- This support also reduces stress and burnout, creating a healthier and more empathetic workplace.

Actively promote and reward empathic actions among leaders and individual contributors to reinforce the importance of empathy.

- Include empathetic behaviors in the annual goals and performance appraisals of leaders and individual contributors.

- Ask specific questions on Employee Satisfaction Surveys to assess the existence of empathic behaviors at the team, leader, and corporate culture levels.

- Recognize and celebrate employees who demonstrate empathy when interacting with colleagues and clients. This recognition can be formal, such as awards or commendations, or informal, like a simple thank-you note.

- Rewarding empathy encourages those behaviors and signals to the organization that empathy is valued and appreciated.

The role of leadership in promoting a culture of empathy cannot be overstated. Leaders must lead by example, demonstrating empathic behaviors in their daily interactions. This includes actively listening to employees, showing genuine concern for their well-being, and addressing their needs and concerns. When leaders model empathy, it sets the tone for the entire organization, encouraging employees to follow suit.

Exercises:

6B. Interactive Element: Developing Team Charters that Emphasize Empathic Values
One practical exercise for building a culture of empathy is developing team charters that emphasize empathic values.

- Gather your team and discuss the importance of empathy in your work. Use a virtual meeting to include remote team members.

- Collaborate to create a charter outlining specific empathic behaviors and values the team commits to upholding. Recommended behaviors include active listening, open communication, and support for each other's well-being.

- Display the charter in a visible place and revisit it regularly to ensure that these values remain a central part of your team's culture.

You can create a supportive and inclusive workplace by prioritizing empathy in every aspect of the organization and implementing practical strategies to foster it. This environment enhances employee well-being and satisfaction and drives organizational success by promoting collaboration, innovation, and trust.

Empathy in Decision-Making: Balance Compassion and Objectivity

Empathy in decision-making is more than just a feel-good concept; it's a practical approach that can profoundly enhance your leadership effectiveness. When you consider the impact of your decisions on employees, stakeholders, and even society, you create more thoughtful and inclusive outcomes.

Take a moment to think about a significant decision you've recently made. Did you consider how it would affect your team members, their families, or the broader community? Balancing emotional insights with logical reasoning allows you to make decisions that are not only practical but also compassionate. This balance ensures that your choices resonate well with those affected and foster a sense of trust and fairness.

Integrating empathy into your decision-making process can be achieved through several practical techniques.

- Use empathic questioning to gather input and perspectives. Before deciding, ask your team how they feel about the potential outcomes. What are their concerns? What are their hopes? This approach provides valuable insights and makes your team feel valued and heard.

- Conduct impact assessments that consider emotional and social factors. Evaluate how your decision will affect the emotional well-being of your employees and the social dynamics within your organization. This assessment helps you anticipate and address potential issues proactively with intelligent Change Management techniques.

- Seek feedback from diverse groups within the organization for a well-rounded perspective. Different departments, roles, and backgrounds can offer unique insights you might not have considered.

- For decisions with broader implications, seek feedback from diverse groups within the community. Understanding how your choices impact external stakeholders, including customers and community members, can provide a more comprehensive view.

This holistic approach ensures that your decisions are inclusive and considerate of all affected parties.

Benefits

Empathic decision-making leads to better outcomes in several ways.

- First, it creates more inclusive and equitable solutions. When you consider diverse perspectives and emotional impacts, you are more likely to develop solutions that meet the needs of various stakeholders.

- This inclusivity builds trust and buy-in from employees and stakeholders, making them more likely to support and commit to the decision.

- Another significant benefit is enhanced effectiveness and sustainability of decisions. Decisions made with empathy are more likely to address the root causes of issues and provide long-term solutions rather than quick fixes.

- Additionally, empathic decision-making builds goodwill in the community. When your organization is considered considerate and socially responsible, it enhances your reputation and fosters positive relationships with external stakeholders.

- This goodwill with external stakeholders can increase customer loyalty, improve community relations, and create a stronger overall brand.

Action Items

Practicing empathic decision-making requires intentional effort and reflection.

Use scenario analysis, a practical activity to assess decisions from multiple perspectives.

- Create hypothetical scenarios and evaluate how different stakeholders might react and feel.
- This exercise helps you anticipate potential issues and develop more balanced solutions.

Use role-playing in your decision-making processes with an emphasis on empathy.

- Partner with a colleague and take turns playing different roles, considering emotional and logical factors in each scenario.
- This practice enhances your ability to integrate empathy into real-life decisions.

Reflect on past decisions and identify opportunities for empathy.

- Think about recent decisions you've made. Were there moments where you could have considered emotional impacts more thoroughly?
- Write down these reflections and consider how you might approach similar decisions differently in the future.
- This ongoing reflection helps you continuously improve your empathic decision-making skills.

Develop decision-making frameworks that incorporate empathy for a structured approach.

- Create guidelines that outline steps for gathering input, conducting impact assessments, and seeking feedback.
- A framework ensures that empathy is consistently integrated into your

decision-making process, making it a natural part of your leadership approach.

Handle Workplace Stress: Techniques for Empathic Leaders

Being an empathic leader comes with its own set of unique stressors. You're not only balancing organizational demands but also juggling your personal well-being. The weight of responsibility can be overwhelming. Managing conflicts and difficult conversations is part of daily life. Every decision you make impacts your team, and the burden of ensuring their well-being falls on your shoulders. Supporting employees through crises and challenges is another constant. Whether it's personal hardships or workplace issues, you're the go-to person for support, making it easy to absorb their stress and feel emotionally drained.

Action Items

Practice mindfulness and stress-reduction techniques to handle this stress effectively.

- Mindfulness helps you stay present and grounded, reducing anxiety and improving focus.

- Simple practices like deep breathing, meditation, or mindful walking can make a big difference.

Set and maintain personal boundaries; this is also crucial. It's easy to blur the lines between work and personal life, especially when your team looks to you for guidance.

- Clearly define your limits and stick to them.

- This might mean not checking emails after a particular time or setting aside specific hours for self-care.

Seek support from mentors, peers, or professional coaches; they can provide invaluable guidance and relief.

- Having someone to talk to who understands your challenges can offer new perspectives and solutions.

- Don't hesitate to reach out for help when you need it.

Prioritize self-care and work-life balance.

- Make time for activities that rejuvenate you, whether exercise, hobbies, or spending time with loved ones.

- Remember, you cannot give from what you do not have. Taking care of yourself is not a luxury but a necessity for effective leadership.

Resilience is vital for empathic leaders in managing workplace stress. Building emotional resilience through self-reflection and self-compassion helps you navigate challenging times gracefully.

- Reflect on your experiences and learn from them.

- Practice self-compassion by treating yourself with the same kindness you offer others.

Foster a resilient mindset through positive thinking and gratitude to transform how you handle adversity.

- Focus on what's going well and acknowledge your achievements.

- Gratitude practices, such as keeping a journal of things you're thankful for, can shift your mindset and improve your overall outlook.

- Embrace positivity. This doesn't mean ignoring challenges but finding strength and motivation in the good things around you.

Exercises:

Practicing stress management and resilience-building exercises can further enhance your ability to cope.

6C. Guided meditation and relaxation techniques are excellent tools.

- Apps like Headspace or Calm offer guided sessions tailored to reducing stress and building resilience.

6D. Journaling about your stressors and coping strategies can provide clarity and insight.

- Write down what's causing stress in you and brainstorm possible solutions.

- Reflect on what's worked in the past and how you can apply those strategies moving forward.

6E. Develop a list of coping strategies for stress; this is crucial.

- Identify what works best for you—physical activity, creative outlets, or relaxation techniques.

- Identify a toolkit of strategies to draw from when stress levels rise. Quick options for coping can make a significant difference.

6F. Engaging in physical activities is a powerful way to reduce stress. Exercise releases endorphins, which improve mood and energy levels.

- Find activities you enjoy, such as running, yoga, strength training, or dancing, and make them a regular part of your routine.

6G. Participating in resilience-building workshops or training sessions will be highly beneficial. These sessions provide structured guidance and support, helping you develop and refine your resilience skills.

As an empathic leader, effectively handling workplace stress is vital for your well-being and the health of your organization. You can manage stress more effectively by practicing mindfulness, setting boundaries, seeking support, and prioritizing self-care. Building emotional resilience through self-reflection, coping strategies, and a positive mindset further equips you to navigate leadership challenges. Embrace these practices and exercises to enhance your resilience and lead with empathy and strength.

Case Studies: Successful Leaders Who Lead with Empathy

Learning from real-life examples can provide both inspiration and practical insights. When we study successful empathic leaders, we see diverse approaches to leadership that emphasize empathy's transformative power. These stories showcase how empathy can shape leadership styles and organizational cultures, offering concrete examples of what works in the real world.

Leader A Case Study: Transforming a Culture

This leader transformed the company's culture through empathy.

- Before their tenure, the organization struggled with high turnover and low employee morale.

- Leader A began by implementing regular one-on-one check-ins with team members to discuss work and understand their personal challenges and aspirations.

- They introduced flexible work arrangements, allowing employees to balance their professional and personal lives better.

- Leader A cultivated a supportive environment by celebrating achievements and providing constructive feedback.

The result? Employee engagement soared, and turnover rates plummeted. The company saw a marked improvement in productivity and innovation as employees felt valued and motivated.

Leader B Case Study: Navigating a Crisis

This leader faced a daunting challenge—leading a team through a crisis. The company had hit a rough patch, with financial instability causing widespread anxiety.

- Instead of resorting to top-down directives, Leader B chose a compassionate approach. They held open forums where employees could voice their concerns and fears.

- Leader B listened actively, acknowledged the emotional toll, and provided transparent updates about the company's efforts to navigate the crisis.

- They offered support resources, including counseling services and stress management workshops.

This empathic leadership helped the team weather the storm and strengthened their trust and loyalty. The company eventually emerged stronger, with a more resilient and united workforce.

Leader C Case Study: Increasing Collaboration and Innovation

Leader C increased collaboration and innovation within the company.

- They encouraged open dialogues and welcomed diverse perspectives, fostering a culture where everyone felt safe to share their ideas.

- Leader C also demonstrated vulnerability and authenticity, sharing personal challenges and learning experiences.

This approach broke down hierarchical barriers and promoted a collaborative spirit. Feeling empowered and supported, the team delivered groundbreaking projects that propelled the company forward.

Lessons Learned

The key takeaways from these case studies are clear.

- Building strong, trust-based relationships with employees is fundamental. When leaders take the time to understand their team's needs and concerns, they create a foundation of trust and respect.

- Creating inclusive and supportive work environments is equally crucial. Policies and practices prioritizing employee well-being and work-life balance foster a sense of belonging and loyalty.

- Demonstrating vulnerability and authenticity in leadership further strengthens these bonds. When leaders share their personal struggles and growth, they humanize themselves, making it easier for employees to relate and connect.

Action Items

Practical lessons from these leaders can be applied to your leadership practices.

- Start by implementing empathy-driven policies and practices.
    - This could include flexible work arrangements, regular check-ins, and support resources for stress and mental health.
- Develop a personal leadership style that emphasizes empathy.
    - Reflect on your interactions and consider how you can listen more actively, show genuine concern, and provide constructive feedback.
    - Encourage and model empathic behaviors within your team. Lead by example, and recognize and reward empathy in others. This reinforces the importance of empathy and cultivates a culture where it thrives.

Summary Points

As we explore these case studies, it's evident that empathy can profoundly impact leadership and organizational success. Integrating empathy into your leadership style can create a more inclusive, supportive, and innovative work environment. This chapter has shown us the power of empathic leadership through real-life examples, demonstrating that empathy is not just a nice-to-have but a critical component of effective leadership.

CHAPTER 7

ACHIEVE EMPATHY IN THE DIGITAL AGE

I magine you're in a virtual meeting with your team, discussing a crucial project. The video boxes flicker on your screen, and you see your colleagues' faces, but something feels off. You notice the lack of energy, the absence of side conversations, and the sterile feeling of interacting through a screen. There's a sense of disconnection that you can't quite shake.

This scenario is all too familiar in our increasingly digital world. While technology has made remote work possible, it has also introduced new challenges for maintaining empathy and connection.

Use Empathic Communication in Virtual Meetings

Virtual communication comes with its unique set of difficulties.

- One of the most significant challenges is the **lack of physical presence and non-verbal cues**. In face-to-face interactions, we rely heavily on body language, facial expressions, and physical proximity to gauge emotions and intentions. These non-verbal cues are often lost in virtual meetings, making understanding and connecting with others harder. Without these subtle signals, it's easy to misinterpret someone's tone or intent, leading to misunderstandings and frustration.

- **Technical issues and distractions** further complicate virtual communication. We've all experienced the dreaded frozen screen or garbled audio that disrupts the flow of conversation. These technical hiccups can make it challenging to stay focused and engaged.

- Additionally, **working from home** can present distractions. Whether it's a barking dog, a ringing doorbell, or the temptation to check your phone, each can distract your attention from the meeting. These interruptions can create a barrier to empathic communication, preventing you from fully tuning in to the conversation.

- The **impersonal nature of screens** adds another layer of difficulty. Interacting through a screen can feel distant and detached, making it harder to establish a genuine connection. The warmth of a smile or the comfort of a reassuring nod is lost when you're separated by pixels. This impersonal feeling can make conveying and receiving empathy challenging, as the human interaction element is diminished.

Despite these challenges, there are practical techniques you can use to enhance empathy in virtual meetings.

- **Actively listen and avoid multitasking**. When you're in a virtual meeting, checking emails, browsing the web, or working on other tasks is tempting. However, multitasking divides your attention and prevents you from fully engaging in the conversation. By focusing solely on the meeting and actively listening to what others say, you can show that you value their input and are genuinely interested in their perspectives.

- **Use clear and concise language** to avoid misunderstandings. The words you choose in virtual communication carry more weight when non-verbal cues are limited. Be mindful of your language and strive to communicate clearly with straightforward sentences. Avoid jargon or ambiguous phrases that could be misinterpreted. Instead, use simple and direct language to convey your message effectively.

- **Encourage participation and acknowledge contributions** to foster a sense of inclusion and connection. In a virtual meeting, it's easy for some voices to get lost or overshadowed. Make a conscious effort to invite input from all participants and acknowledge their contributions. This can be as simple as saying, "Thank you for sharing your thoughts," or "I appreciate your perspective." By recognizing and valuing everyone's input, you create a more inclusive and empathetic environment.

- **Use the virtual meeting's chat space for side conversations**, rather than separate private chats, so that there are no hidden agendas and relevant side chats can be brought to the team's attention.

Visual and auditory cues are vital in conveying empathy in virtual settings.

- For example, maintaining eye contact through the camera can help simulate a direct connection. If you do not engage your video in meetings, reconsider and turn it on. While it might feel awkward initially, look into the camera rather than at the screen to make the other person feel like you're engaging with them. Use facial expressions and gestures to show engagement. A nod, a smile, or even raising your eyebrows in interest can convey that you're actively listening and invested in the conversation.

- Modulating your tone of voice and pace can also convey understanding and empathy. Speak in a calm and measured tone, vary your pitch, and pause to allow others to respond to make your communication more empathetic. This approach shows you're thoughtful and considerate, enhancing the emotional connection.

- Another practical step is to ensure good lighting and sound quality. Clear communication is essential for empathy, and good lighting helps convey facial expressions, while clear audio ensures that your voice is heard without distortion.

Exercises

Consider engaging in specific exercises to practice and improve your empathic communication skills in virtual settings.

7A. Practice role-playing with virtual meeting scenarios and a focus on empathy.

- Partner with a colleague or friend and simulate different meeting scenarios, such as discussing a project update or resolving a conflict.

- Focus on actively listening, using clear language, and employing visual and auditory cues to convey empathy.

- After each role-play, provide feedback to each other on what worked well and what could be improved.

7B. Record and review virtual meetings for valuable information.

- With permission, record your virtual meetings and replay them to identify areas for improvement.

- Pay attention to your body language, facial expressions, and tone of voice. Are you making eye contact through the camera? Are you using gestures to show engagement? Are you speaking clearly and concisely?

- Reflect on these aspects and make adjustments to enhance your empathic communication.

7C. Practice active listening and reflective responses in virtual meetings.

- During your next virtual meeting, consciously listen actively and reflect on what you hear. For example, suppose a colleague shares a concern about making timely progress. In that case, you might respond, "I hear you're frustrated about the project timeline. Let's discuss how we can address this."

- This approach shows that you're listening, understanding, and validating their feelings.

Empathic communication in virtual meetings is challenging but not impossible. By actively listening, using clear language, encouraging participation, and employing visual and auditory cues, you can enhance your empathic abilities and build stronger connections, even via a video screen. These techniques and exercises will help you navigate the complexities of virtual communication, making your interactions more meaningful and empathetic.

Navigate Social Media with Empathy: Best Practices

If you've ever found yourself scrolling through your social media feed, feeling a mix of emotions from the barrage of posts, comments, and reactions, you're not alone. Social media has transformed how we communicate, but it has also introduced unique challenges for practicing empathy.

- One of the most significant challenges is the anonymity and detachment that online interactions often foster. When you're behind a screen, it's easy to forget there's an actual person on the other side. This detachment can make it difficult to connect on a human level, leading to misunderstandings and a lack of empathy.

- The prevalence of negative and hostile behavior on social media further complicates things. Trolls, keyboard warriors, and the general outrage culture can create a toxic environment where empathy is scarce.

- The anonymity of the internet encourages people to say things they might never say face-to-face, contributing to a cycle of negativity. This hostile behavior affects the targets of these attacks. It creates a broader atmosphere of distrust and defensiveness, making engaging in meaningful, empathetic conversations challenging.

- Another issue is the rapid pace and volume of information on social media. With endless posts, tweets, and updates flooding your feed, it's easy to become overwhelmed. This information overload can make it difficult to focus on any interaction long enough to practice genuine empathy. Instead of taking the time to understand and connect, you might find yourself skimming through content, missing the nuances crucial for empathy.

- The constant barrage of information can also desensitize you to the emotions and experiences of others, reducing your capacity for empathy over time.

Despite these challenges, there are practical methods to enhance empathy while using social media.

- Use positive and supportive language. Words have power, and choosing to use them thoughtfully can make a significant difference. Instead of jumping to criticize or argue, try to offer encouragement and support. Compliment someone on their achievements, express gratitude for their insights, or acknowledge their feelings. Positive language fosters a more empathetic and supportive online community.

- Avoid engaging in or perpetuating negative behavior. When you come across hostile comments or inflammatory posts, responding in kind is tempting. However, this only fuels the cycle of negativity. Instead, choose to disengage from toxic interactions or, if appropriate, offer a calm and reasoned response. By not contributing to the negativity, you help create a more respectful and empathetic online environment. Remember, silence can be powerful, too. Sometimes, the best response is no response at all.

- Take the time to understand different perspectives before responding. Social media often feels like an echo chamber, where you only encounter opinions and viewpoints similar to your own. Hearing only the confirmations of like-minded people can hinder empathy, as it limits your exposure to diverse experiences and perspectives.

- When you come across a post or comment that challenges your views, take a moment to consider the other person's perspective. Ask yourself why they might feel that way, what experiences might have shaped their views, and how you can engage with them respectfully. This reflection can help you respond with empathy rather than defensiveness.

Managing emotional tone in writing is especially critical in digital communication, where non-verbal cues are absent, to influence how messages are perceived.

- **Be Mindful of Word Choice**: Words can convey warmth, coldness, acceptance, or judgment. Choose words that convey understanding and openness, even when you disagree. For example, phrases like "I see your point" or "That's an interesting perspective" can help maintain a constructive tone.

- **Use Emojis Wisely**: Emojis can help clarify tone but should be used judiciously. A smile or a thoughtful face can soften a message and show warmth. However, it's essential to match the emoji to the seriousness of the conversation. Overusing them or using inappropriate emojis can undermine your message.

- **Reflect Before Responding**: Pause, especially if the message evokes strong emotions. This pause can temper immediate reactions and allow for a more considered response that reflects empathy rather than impulsivity.

- **Clarify Your Intentions**: In cases where tone might be misunderstood, it's helpful to be explicit about your intentions. For example, you could start a response with, "I want to understand your position better…" or "My goal is to share a different perspective, not to criticize…"

- **Adopt a Curious Stance**: Approaching conversations with curiosity rather than defensiveness can transform the tone of your interactions. Phrases like "Can you tell me more about that…" or "I'm curious to hear why you think that…" invite open dialogue and signal a willingness to understand rather than confront.

- **Practice Reflective Affirmation**: When replying, briefly summarize or affirm what the other person has said before adding your viewpoint. This shows that you are listening and value their input, which can defuse potential defensiveness. For example, "I understand that you feel strongly about this, and I appreciate your perspective. Here's another angle that might be worth considering…"

- **Avoid Caps Lock and Excessive Punctuation**: Writing in all caps or using multiple exclamation points can come across as shouting or aggression. Use standard capitalization and punctuation to maintain a calm and respectful tone.

Benefits

Practicing empathy online is not just about improving individual interactions; it has a broader impact on the social media environment.

- Building positive and supportive online communities contributes to a culture of empathy and understanding. These communities can become safe spaces where people feel valued and heard, fostering a sense of belonging and connection.

- Reducing conflict and promoting respectful dialogue are also critical. Conflicts are more likely to be constructively resolved when empathy is present, and discussions become opportunities for growth rather than battlegrounds.

- Encouraging authentic and meaningful connections is another significant benefit of practicing digital empathy. Social media often promotes superficial interactions, where likes and shares replace genuine engagement. By taking the time to connect on a deeper level, you can build more fulfilling and impactful relationships. Share your experiences, ask thoughtful questions, and show genuine interest in others' lives. These authentic interactions can transform your social media experience, making it a platform for genuine connection rather than just a content stream.

Exercises

Consider engaging in specific activities to practice and develop your empathic skills on social media.

7D. Reflect on past social media interactions as an exercise.

- Think about your recent posts, comments, and messages. Were there moments where you could have been more empathetic?

- Identify these opportunities and consider how you might respond differently next time.

- This reflection helps you become more mindful of your online behavior and more intentional in your interactions.

7E. Create and share positive and supportive content.

- Use your social media presence to spread kindness and encouragement.

- Share uplifting stories, express gratitude, and highlight the achievements of others.

- This positive content can inspire and uplift your followers, contributing to a more empathetic online community.

7F. Engage in thoughtful and respectful discussions.

- When you encounter differing opinions, approach the conversation with curiosity and respect.

- Ask questions, listen actively, and seek to understand rather than to win the argument.

- These discussions can become opportunities for learning and connection.

7G. Spend a week focusing on empathy in your social media interactions.

- Each day, choose one interaction and make a conscious effort to respond with empathy. It could be a supportive comment on a friend's post, a thoughtful question in a discussion, or a private message expressing gratitude.

- At the end of the week, reflect on these interactions. How did it feel to practice empathy online? How did it impact your relationships and overall social media experience?

- This exercise can help you integrate empathy into your online presence, making it a natural part of your social media interactions.

Navigating social media with empathy is challenging, but it's also gratifying. By using positive language, avoiding negative behavior, and taking the time to understand different perspectives, you can transform your social media experience.

Practicing digital empathy improves interactions and contributes to a more positive and supportive online environment. You can develop your empathic skills and create meaningful connections through reflection and intentional practice, even in the digital world.

Digital Detox: Balance Online Presence and Emotional Well-being

You've probably heard the term "digital detox" tossed around, but what does it mean?

DEFINITION: A digital detox is about taking a break from screens and reducing online activity.

Think of it as hitting the reset button on your digital habits. In today's world, where our phones are practically glued to our hands, a digital detox can be a game-changer for your emotional well-being.

- Reducing screen time and online activity gives your mind a much-needed break. Constant notifications, endless scrolling, and the pressure to stay updated can be overwhelming. By stepping away, you allow your brain to relax and recharge. This break can alleviate stress and improve your mental health, making you feel more present and less anxious.

- Reconnecting with the physical world and personal relationships is another crucial aspect of a digital detox. When you're constantly online, you miss out on the real-life experiences happening around you.

Whether it's a walk in the park, a conversation with a loved one, or simply enjoying a meal without distractions, these moments can bring immense joy and fulfillment. By disconnecting from your screens, you open up space for these meaningful interactions, strengthening your relationships and enhancing your overall quality of life.

Action Items

But how do you go about implementing a digital detox?

- One effective method is setting specific times for your detox periods. For example, designate weekends as tech-free zones or choose certain daily hours to go offline. This approach helps create a routine, making sticking to your detox plan easier. These designated times quickly become something you look forward to, a sanctuary from the constant buzz of digital life.

- Creating tech-free zones and activities can also support your detox efforts. Designate areas in your home where screens are off-limits, like the bedroom or dining room. Fill these spaces with activities that don't involve screens, such as reading, gardening, or playing board games. These tech-free zones become havens of calm and connection, offering a respite from the digital world.

- Another powerful technique is practicing mindfulness and being present in offline interactions. When you're with family or friends, consciously put your phone away and focus on the moment. Engage fully in conversations, listen actively, and notice the nuances of the interaction. This mindful approach enhances relationships and deepens your appreciation for the present moment.

BENEFITS

- Reducing digital distractions can significantly enhance your empathic abilities. When you're not constantly checking your phone or thinking about your next social media post, you can focus more fully on the people around you. This improved focus and attentiveness in interactions makes it easier to pick up on subtle emotional cues, fostering a deeper understanding and connection.

- Another benefit of digital detox is enhancing emotional regulation and awareness. When you're not bombarded by constant stimuli, you have more mental space to process your emotions and reflect on your feelings. This heightened self-awareness allows you to regulate your emotions more effectively, making you more empathetic to others' experiences.

- Fostering deeper and more meaningful connections is the most rewarding aspect of a digital detox. When fully present and engaged in your interactions, you create a space where genuine connection can flourish. These deeper connections enrich your relationships, making them more satisfying.

EXERCISES

Consider engaging in specific exercises to help you implement and maintain a digital detox.

7H. Start by planning and scheduling regular detox periods.

- Mark these times on your calendar and treat them as non-negotiable appointments with yourself.

- Whether it's a daily hour of tech-free time or an entire weekend offline, these scheduled breaks become anchors for your well-being.

7I. Engage in offline hobbies and activities that promote well-being.

- Rediscover passions that don't involve screens, such as painting, hiking, or cooking.

- These activities provide a break from digital distractions and offer a sense of accomplishment and joy.

7J. Reflect on the impact of your digital detox on emotional health and relationships.

- After each detox period, take a few moments to journal about your experience.

- How did it feel to be offline? What did you notice about your emotions and interactions? Did you feel more connected to yourself and others?

- This reflection helps reinforce the benefits of your detox and motivates you to continue the practice.

Summary Points

In our digitally saturated world, a digital detox can be a powerful tool for enhancing empathy and emotional well-being. By reducing screen time, reconnecting with the physical world, and practicing mindfulness, you create space for deeper connections and greater self-awareness. These benefits extend beyond the individual, fostering a more empathetic and connected society. As we navigate the complexities of modern life, balancing our online presence with our emotional well-being becomes not just a choice but a necessity.

CHAPTER 8

NAVIGATE DIFFICULT RELATIONSHIPS

P icture this: you're at a family reunion, and your cousin, who has always been the center of attention, starts boasting about their latest accomplishments. The conversation quickly becomes a monologue about how amazing they are, how everyone else is inferior, and how their life is a series of unparalleled successes.

You try to steer the conversation toward a more balanced exchange, but your cousin's need for admiration and lack of interest in anyone else's experiences make it impossible. This encounter is a classic example of dealing with a narcissist, and it's just one of the many challenging relationships we face in life.

Identify Narcissists, Sociopaths, and Psychopaths

Understanding difficult personalities is crucial for navigating these complex relationships. Narcissism, sociopathy, and psychopathy are distinct yet often misunderstood.

DEFINITION: Narcissism involves excessive self-focus, a constant need for admiration, and a glaring lack of empathy.

Narcissists are typically preoccupied with fantasies of unlimited success, power, and brilliance. They believe they are special and unique, deserving of excessive admiration and preferential treatment. This sense of entitlement often leads to exploitative relationships where the narcissist takes advantage of others to achieve their own ends.

DEFINITION: Sociopathy is characterized by antisocial behavior, impulsivity, and a lack of remorse.

Sociopaths often engage in deceitful and manipulative behaviors, showing little regard for social norms or the rights of others. They are pathological liars, frequently changing their stories to suit their needs. Their impulsivity leads them to take unnecessary risks without considering the consequences, and they often display aggressive behavior.

Unlike narcissists, who can sometimes show empathy when it serves their purposes, sociopaths generally have a deeper incapacity for genuine emotional connection.

DEFINITION: Psychopathy is marked by superficial charm, manipulativeness, and emotional shallowness.

Psychopaths are master manipulators, using their charm to deceive and control others. They lack guilt and remorse, making engaging in harmful behaviors easy without emotional repercussions.

Psychopaths are often calculated and methodical in their deceit, planning their actions meticulously to achieve their goals. Their emotional shallowness means they can mimic emotions but do not truly experience them, making their interactions feel hollow and insincere.

Identifying Empathy-Deficient People

Recognizing these behaviors can help you identify when dealing with an empathy-deficient individual.

- Narcissists exhibit grandiosity, a sense of entitlement, and exploitative relationships. They crave constant admiration and are often envious of others.

- Sociopaths show pathological lying, disregard for social norms, and aggressive behavior. They are manipulative and lack genuine emotional responses.

- Psychopaths display calculated deception, emotional shallowness, and high impulsivity. They are charming on the surface but lack the depth of genuine emotional connection.

Examples

Let's explore some real-life scenarios to illustrate these traits.

- Imagine working for a narcissistic boss who constantly undermines employees to maintain control. They take credit for others' work, dismiss contributions, and belittle team members to inflate their sense of superiority. This creates a toxic work environment where employees feel undervalued and demoralized.

- Now, consider a sociopathic colleague who manipulates team members for personal gain. They lie about their qualifications, fabricate stories to pit colleagues against each other, and take risky actions without considering the consequences. Their behavior creates chaos and mistrust within the team, making collaborating difficult.

- Lastly, think about a psychopathic partner who exhibits controlling and deceitful behavior. They charm you with their seemingly perfect demeanor, but their manipulative tactics become apparent over time. They isolate you from friends and family, lie about their past, and show no remorse for their actions. The emotional shallowness and lack of guilt make having a genuine, trusting relationship challenging.

Impacts

Interactions with empathy-deficient individuals can have a profound impact on empaths.

- The constant emotional drain leads to exhaustion and burnout.

- When you continually try to understand and connect with someone who lacks empathy, you can erode your self-esteem and self-worth.

- You start questioning your perceptions and feelings, doubting your ability to navigate relationships.

- The stress and anxiety of dealing with these individuals can also take a toll on your mental and physical health.

- You may experience increased anxiety, difficulty sleeping, and a constant sense of tension.

Understanding the nature of narcissism, sociopathy, and psychopathy is the first step in handling these difficult relationships. Recognizing the behavioral traits and red flags can help you navigate interactions more effectively. By being aware of these relationships' impact on your well-being, you can take proactive steps to protect yourself and maintain your emotional health. Remember, it's not about changing the other person but about understanding and managing your interactions with them to preserve your well-being and sanity.

Use Strategies to Deal with Narcissists: Protect Your Energy

Navigating relationships with narcissists can be incredibly draining, especially for empaths who naturally absorb the emotions of those around them. Protecting your energy is crucial to avoid emotional depletion and maintain stability and well-being. When you constantly give without receiving genuine emotional support in return, you risk burnout. Your mental and emotional reserves get depleted, leaving you feeling exhausted and overwhelmed. This is why energy protection is not a luxury but a necessity for overall health.

Limit interactions and set clear time boundaries to protect your energy.

- If you know specific encounters will be draining, keep them short. Plan your time wisely and allocate no more time than you can emotionally afford.

- For example, if you have a narcissistic family member, perhaps limit visits to short, manageable periods and ensure you have a clear exit strategy.

Visualize protective barriers.

- Imagine yourself surrounded by a bubble or shield that keeps negative energy out.

- This mental imagery can create a psychological buffer, helping you feel more secure and less affected by the narcissist's behavior.

Practice detachment.

- This doesn't mean becoming cold or unfeeling; it's about not taking things personally.

- Narcissists often use manipulative tactics to provoke emotional reactions. By recognizing these tactics for what they are, you can choose not to engage emotionally.

- Focus on the objective facts of the situation rather than getting swept up in the emotional drama.

- Keep your interactions brief and to the point. This minimizes opportunities for the narcissist to manipulate the conversation and drain your energy.

Maintain emotional distance and detachment to protect yourself from the manipulative tactics that narcissists often employ.

- Recognize when you're being baited into an emotional response and choose to respond with calm, factual statements instead.

- For example, suppose a narcissistic colleague tries to provoke you by belittling your work. Rather than reacting defensively, you might say, "I appreciate your feedback. I'll consider it."

- This keeps the interaction professional and short without giving them the emotional reaction they seek.

Keep interactions focused on objective facts to help you stay grounded.

- Stick to the facts instead of getting entangled in arguments or emotional exchanges.

- If a narcissist tries to twist the conversation to make you doubt yourself, calmly reiterate the facts.

- This approach protects your energy and reinforces your boundaries. It shows you won't be easily manipulated or drawn into their emotional games.

Exercises

8A. Visualization Exercise: Creating Mental Barriers

- Take a few minutes each day to practice this visualization exercise.

- Sit comfortably and close your eyes.

- Imagine a strong, protective bubble surrounding you. This bubble is impenetrable to negative energy. Visualize it as vividly as possible, seeing its color and feeling its texture.

- As you go through your day, imagine this bubble around you, keeping you safe from draining interactions.

- Reflect on how this makes you feel and impacts your energy levels.

8B. Reflection exercises can also be beneficial.

- After interacting with a narcissist, take some time to reflect on the encounter.

- Identify any emotional triggers you experienced and consider how you could handle similar situations in the future.

- This reflection helps you understand your emotional responses and develop strategies to protect your energy more effectively.

8C. Practice assertive communication.

- Use "I" statements to express your needs and boundaries clearly.

- For example, "I need some time to think about this," or "I'm not comfortable discussing this topic."

- Assertive communication helps you maintain your boundaries without escalating the situation. It shows that you respect yourself and your needs, which is crucial when dealing with narcissists who often try to undermine your confidence.

By incorporating these techniques into your interactions, you can create a protective barrier that shields you from the draining effects of narcissistic behavior. This allows you to maintain your emotional stability and well-being, ensuring you have the energy and resilience to navigate these challenging relationships effectively.

Stay Grounded Around Sociopaths with Effective Communication

Interacting with sociopaths presents unique challenges that can leave you feeling mentally and emotionally drained.

- These individuals are often manipulative and deceitful, using lies and cunning tactics to get what they want.

- They lack genuine emotional responses, which makes it challenging to connect with them on any meaningful level.

- Instead of displaying true feelings, they may mimic emotions to manipulate those around them.

- This emotional shallowness, combined with a tendency to provoke and escalate conflicts, makes dealing with sociopaths particularly taxing.

- They might bait you into arguments or create chaos to distract you from their shortcomings, leaving you bewildered and upset.

Communicating effectively with sociopaths requires a strategic approach.

Use clear, concise, and factual language.

- When you state facts plainly, you reduce the room for manipulation.

Avoid emotional engagement.

- Stay neutral and composed, even when they try to provoke an emotional reaction.

- This helps you maintain control of the conversation and prevents them from gaining the upper hand.

Set firm boundaries and stick to them.

- Clearly define what is acceptable and what is not, and don't waver.

- This consistency helps you maintain your integrity and protects you from their manipulative tactics.

Stay grounded; this is essential when dealing with sociopaths.

- Maintain a calm and composed stance to prevent emotional manipulation and keep you focused.

Practice mindfulness.

- This will help you stay present and centered, making it easier to respond thoughtfully rather than impulsively.

Use deep breathing or progressive muscle relaxation techniques in these moments.

- Use grounding techniques, like feeling the sensation of your feet on the floor or holding a small object, to anchor yourself in the present and provide a sense of stability.

These practices help you stay emotionally centered, reducing the impact of the sociopath's attempts to unsettle you.

EXERCISES

8D. Role-Playing Exercise: Practicing Neutral Responses
Role-playing can be a valuable tool for developing your ability to stay grounded when communicating with sociopaths.

- Partner with a friend and create scenarios based on real-life interactions you've experienced or anticipate.

- Practice responding with clear, concise, and factual language. Focus on maintaining a neutral tone, avoiding emotional engagement.

- After each role-play, discuss what worked well and what could be improved.

- This exercise helps you build confidence and prepares you for actual encounters.

8E. Mindfulness exercises can further enhance your emotional stability.

- Spend a few minutes each day practicing mindfulness meditation.

- Focus on your breath, noticing the sensation of air entering and leaving your body.

- When your mind wanders, gently bring it back to your breath.

- This practice trains your mind to stay present, making it easier to remain calm and centered during challenging interactions. Over time, you'll find it easier to maintain your composure, even when dealing with the most challenging individuals.

8F. Journal reflections on your communication experiences for valuable insights.

- After interacting with a sociopath, take some time to write about the encounter.

- Reflect on how you felt, how you responded, and what you could do differently next time.

- This self-reflection helps you identify interaction patterns and develop more effective strategies. It also allows you to process your emotions, reducing the lingering impact of these challenging encounters.

Incorporating these techniques and exercises into your daily routine can significantly improve your ability to communicate effectively with sociopaths. You protect yourself from manipulation by using clear, concise language, avoiding emotional engagement, and setting firm boundaries. Staying grounded through mindfulness and grounding techniques ensures you remain composed and focused.

Role-playing scenarios and journaling reflections further enhance your skills, preparing you for real-life interactions. These strategies empower you to navigate challenging relationships with confidence and resilience, preserving your well-being and emotional stability.

Maintain Vigilance Around Psychopaths: Developing Effective Defense Mechanisms

Navigating relationships with psychopaths presents its own unique set of challenges, as these individuals are often exceptionally skilled at manipulation and deception. They utilize their superficial charm to gain trust and exploit it without remorse. Developing effective defense mechanisms is crucial for maintaining your mental and emotional well-being when dealing with psychopaths.

Recognize the Red Flags.

- The first step in protecting yourself is to become adept at recognizing the signs of psychopathic behavior.
- This includes superficial charm, a grandiose sense of self-worth, pathological lying, and a lack of empathy.
- Awareness of these traits can help you maintain a healthy skepticism and prevent you from falling into their manipulative traps.

Keep Your Interactions Impersonal and Fact-Based.

- When you must interact with a psychopath, strive to keep the exchange as impersonal and fact-based as possible.
- Avoid sharing personal details or emotional reactions, which they can use against you.
- Focus on practical matters and keep your communications brief and to the point to avoid giving them leverage.

Establish and Enforce Strict Boundaries.

- Clear boundaries are vital when dealing with a psychopath.
- Decide in advance what behaviors you will not tolerate and be prepared to enforce these boundaries firmly.
- If a psychopath tries to overstep, reassert your limits without hesitation

or guilt.

- Consistency is vital in ensuring they understand that their manipulative tactics are ineffective with you.

Document Everything.

- Given their propensity for lying and manipulating facts, keep a detailed record of all your interactions with a psychopath.

- This can be invaluable when you need to prove a point or defend your actions, particularly in a professional environment.

Seek External Support.

- Dealing with psychopaths can be isolating and overwhelming. It's important to have a support system in place, whether it's friends, family, or professionals who understand your situation.

- They can provide not only emotional support but also a second opinion on your interactions with the psychopath, helping you stay grounded in reality.

Prioritize Your Safety.

- If at any point you feel your safety is compromised, prioritize protective measures.

- Psychopaths can be unpredictable and dangerous, especially if they feel their control slipping away.

- Do not hesitate to seek help from authorities or professional services offering protection and advice.

Engage in Self-Care.

- Regular self-care practices are essential when dealing with the draining effects of a psychopathic relationship.

- Engage in activities that replenish your energy and provide a respite from stress, such as exercise, meditation, or hobbies you enjoy.

- Keeping yourself mentally and physically healthy is crucial for resilience in challenging situations.

EXERCISES

8G. Scenario Analysis Exercise

- Reflect on past interactions with individuals who exhibited psychopathic traits.

- Consider what red flags were present and how you responded.

- Think about what you could do differently in the future to protect yourself.

- This exercise helps develop a quicker response to similar red flags in the future.

8H. Mindfulness and Grounding Techniques

- Practice mindfulness exercises daily to enhance your emotional regulation and reduce susceptibility to manipulation.

- Techniques such as focused breathing, mindfulness meditation, or sensory awareness exercises can help maintain your emotional equilibrium.

Incorporating these strategies and exercises into your routine can help you manage interactions with psychopaths more effectively. By maintaining vigilance and prioritizing your mental health, you can protect yourself from their harmful behaviors and minimize their impact on your life.

SET BOUNDARIES WITH EMPATHY-DEFICIENT INDIVIDUALS

Navigating relationships with empathy-deficient individuals can be daunting, especially when their behaviors constantly test your limits. Establishing firm boundaries is crucial in these interactions. It's about protecting your emotional and mental well-being, preventing manipulation and exploitation, and maintaining your personal autonomy and control.

Without clear boundaries, you may find yourself constantly drained, feeling like your needs are secondary to these individuals' demands and manipulations. Setting firm boundaries creates a protective barrier that ensures your well-being comes first.

Clearly define your personal limits and non-negotiables when dealing with empathy-deficient individuals.

- Take some time to reflect on what behaviors you can and cannot tolerate.

- Write them down if it helps. This clarity will serve as your foundation when communicating your boundaries.

- For example, if you're dealing with a colleague who constantly interrupts your work with their demands, decide when you are available for such interruptions and stick to those times.

- Communicating these boundaries assertively and directly is essential. Use "I" statements to express your needs clearly and without ambiguity. For example, "I need uninterrupted time from 9 AM to 11 AM to focus on my tasks. Let's discuss any issues after that." This approach is both respectful and firm.

Enforce your boundaries consistently despite resistance. This is where the real challenge lies.

- Empathy-deficient individuals are often skilled at pushing back and guilt-tripping to get what they want. It's important to recognize these tactics and not give in to the pressure.

- When you set a boundary, expect some resistance and have a plan for how you will respond.

- It might be helpful to rehearse what you will say and how you will handle pushback.

- Stay calm and stick to your script.

- Consistently enforcing your boundaries will reinforce them over time, making it clear that you are serious about protecting your space and well-being.

Deal with pushback and guilt-tripping, a common challenge in boundary-setting.

- These individuals may accuse you of being selfish or uncaring for setting limits. They may try to manipulate your feelings to get you to relent.

- It's crucial to stay firm and not let guilt sway your decisions.

- Remember that setting boundaries is not about being harsh or unkind; it's about taking care of yourself.

Recognize and address boundary violations promptly.

- If someone oversteps, address it immediately.

- Let them know that their behavior is unacceptable, and reiterate your boundaries.

- Stay firm, and don't give in to pressure.

- The more consistent you are, the more likely they will respect your boundaries over time.

Exercises

Practice boundary-setting to help you become more comfortable and confident in enforcing your limits.

81. Role-playing boundary-setting conversations with a trusted friend or therapist can be incredibly helpful.

- Practice different scenarios where you must set boundaries and have your friend act as the empathy-deficient individual.

- This will allow you to rehearse your responses and receive feedback on your approach.

- If your challenge is with a long-distance manager, teammate, or subordinate at work, or even a long-distance friend or relative, practice this role-playing over a virtual meeting.

8J. Reflecting on past boundary violations and identifying strategies for improvement is another helpful exercise.

- Think about times when your boundaries were crossed and how you handled it.

- What worked? What didn't?

- Use these reflections to refine your approach.

8K. Creating a personal boundary plan for different relationships can provide a clear roadmap for maintaining your limits.

- Identify the specific boundaries you must set with family members, colleagues, friends, and others.

- Write down your boundaries and the strategies you will use to enforce them.

- This plan can serve as a reference guide when you face challenging situations, helping you stay grounded and focused on protecting your well-being.

Protect Yourself: Techniques for Empaths in Toxic Relationships

Imagine being in a relationship where every interaction leaves you feeling drained and anxious. This is a common experience for empaths in toxic relationships. Self-protection becomes crucial in these situations. It's not just about surviving but thriving despite the negativity around you. Protecting yourself prevents emotional and psychological harm, allowing you to maintain personal well-being and resilience.

Practice self-care and prioritize personal needs as a foundational self-protection technique.

- As an empath, you naturally prioritize others' needs over your own. However, it's essential to carve out time for yourself.

- Engage in activities that rejuvenate you, whether reading a book, taking a walk, or indulging in a hobby.

- Make self-care a non-negotiable part of your routine. This will replenish your emotional reserves and reinforce the message that your well-being is important.

Limit exposure to toxic individuals and environments.

- If possible, reduce the time you spend with toxic people.

- This might mean setting limits on how often you interact with them.

- It might mean spending time in environments where you feel supported and safe. This helps create a buffer, reducing the emotional impact of their negativity.

Seek support from trusted friends, family, or professionals.

- Talking to someone who understands your situation can provide much-needed validation and guidance.

- Whether it's a close friend, a family member, or a therapist, having a support system helps you navigate the challenges of toxic relationships.

- These individuals can offer a different perspective, helping you see things more clearly and objectively.

- They can also provide practical advice on how to handle specific situations, making you feel less isolated.

Use self-awareness and self-reflection to play a pivotal role in enhancing self-protection.

- Recognizing your personal triggers and vulnerabilities allows you to anticipate and manage your reactions.

- For example, if you know that specific topics or behaviors trigger an emotional response, you can prepare yourself mentally and emotionally to handle them.

Understand your own emotional needs and boundaries.

- Take time to reflect on what you need to feel safe and supported. This understanding helps you set and enforce boundaries more effectively.

Reflect on past experiences to identify patterns and lessons.

- Look back at your interactions with toxic individuals.

- What worked? What didn't?

- Use these insights to inform your future actions.

Exercises

8L. Keep a Self-Care Journal.

- Each day, jot down how you're feeling, what self-care activities you engaged in, and any interactions with toxic individuals.

- Reflect on how these interactions affected you and what measures you took to protect yourself.

- This journaling practice helps you track your well-being and identify patterns.

- Over time, you'll better understand what works best for you, allowing you to fine-tune your self-protection strategies.

8M. Reflect on interactions with toxic individuals to gain valuable insights.

- After each interaction, take a moment to think about how you felt and what triggered those feelings.

- Did you feel drained, anxious, or upset?

- What specifically caused those emotions?

- Identifying these triggers helps you develop strategies to protect yourself in future interactions. For example, if certain behaviors or comments consistently upset you, you can mentally prepare to handle or avoid them altogether.

8N, Practice mindfulness and grounding techniques to stay centered.

- Mindfulness involves staying present and fully engaged in the moment, which helps you manage stress and anxiety.

- Techniques like deep breathing, progressive muscle relaxation, or focusing on your senses can ground you and reduce the impact of negative interactions.

- These practices help you stay calm and composed, making it easier to navigate toxic relationships without getting overwhelmed.

Summary Points

By incorporating these self-protection techniques into your daily life, you can navigate toxic relationships more effectively. Practicing self-care, limiting exposure to negativity, seeking support, and enhancing self-awareness all contribute to a stronger, more resilient you.

Keeping a self-care journal and reflecting on interactions helps you understand and manage your emotional responses, while mindfulness and grounding techniques keep you centered. These strategies empower you to protect your well-being, ensuring you thrive even in the most challenging relationships.

CHAPTER 9

COMMIT TO EMPATHY FOR PERSONAL GROWTH

One evening, I felt utterly overwhelmed by work and life demands. I was sitting on my sofa, staring blankly at the wall, feeling completely drained, when my phone buzzed with a message from a friend seeking advice. At that moment, I realized I had nothing left to give.

That's when it hit me: I was disconnected from my emotions. I had been so focused on others that I had lost touch with myself. This moment of clarity led me to explore the profound connection between empathy and self-awareness.

Use Empathy as a Path to Self-Awareness: Reflective Practices

Empathy is often seen as an outward-focused skill, but it also has a powerful inward dimension.

- You can deepen your self-awareness by tuning into your emotions and understanding their origins.

- This means recognizing how your feelings arise and affect your actions and words.

- For example, if you feel frustrated after a difficult conversation, take a moment to reflect. What triggered that frustration?

- Understanding these emotional triggers can provide valuable insights into your behavior and help you grow.

When you become aware of your emotions, you also see how your actions impact others. This is crucial for personal growth.

- If you snap at a colleague during a stressful day, recognizing your emotional state can lead to an apology and a more thoughtful approach in the future.

- This awareness fosters better relationships as you learn to navigate your emotions and their effects on those around you.

- Moreover, it opens the door to identifying your strengths and areas for growth. Understanding your emotional patterns allows you to leverage your strengths and work on your weaknesses.

Exercises

Reflective practices are essential for enhancing self-awareness through empathy.

9A. Start with daily reflection exercises.

- At the end of each day, take a few minutes to review your interactions and emotions.
- Ask yourself questions like, "What emotions did I feel today and why?" and "How did my actions affect those around me?"
- This simple practice can reveal patterns and provide clarity.

9B. Another powerful tool is practicing self-empathy.

- When you experience intense emotions, take a moment to sit with them without judgment.
- Acknowledge your feelings and try to understand their roots.
- This practice not only enhances self-awareness but also builds emotional resilience.

9C. Seeking feedback from trusted friends or mentors can also be incredibly enlightening.

- Sometimes, others can see patterns in our behavior that we miss.
- Ask for honest feedback about how you handle emotions and interact with others.
- This can be a humbling experience but a valuable step toward personal growth.
- Use this feedback to gain new perspectives and make adjustments where needed.

Benefits

The benefits of self-awareness for personal growth are immense.

- Improved emotional regulation is one of the most significant advantages. When you understand your emotions, you can respond to situations more calmly and rationally. This resilience enables you to navigate life's challenges with greater ease.

- Another benefit is enhanced relationships. By understanding yourself better, you communicate more effectively and empathetically, fostering deeper connections with others.

- Additionally, self-awareness brings greater clarity to your personal goals and aspirations. When you know what drives you and what holds you back, you can set more meaningful goals and work toward them with confidence.

Exercises

9D. Consider journaling prompts focused on daily experiences and emotions to practice reflective self-awareness.

- Write about a significant interaction each day and explore the emotions involved.

- What did you feel? Why did you feel that way?

- How did it affect your actions?

9E. Reflective meditation practices are also beneficial.

- Spend a few minutes each day in quiet reflection, focusing on your inner thoughts and feelings.

- This mindfulness practice can enhance your self-awareness and emotional regulation.

9F. Self-assessment quizzes can be a fun and insightful way to identify personal traits and tendencies.

- Create a unique quiz with questions exploring your emotional responses and behaviors.

- Use the results to pinpoint areas for further reflection and growth.

- These exercises can provide a structured approach to developing self-awareness and integrating empathy into your personal growth journey.

9G. Reflective Journaling Prompt

- Take a moment to reflect on a recent interaction where you felt a strong emotion.

- Write about the situation, your emotional response, and the underlying reasons for that emotion.

- Consider how your actions affected the other person and what you can learn from this experience.

- How can you apply this insight to future interactions?

Developing self-awareness through empathy is a transformative process. It requires intentional reflection, self-compassion, and a willingness to grow. By embracing these practices, you can enhance your emotional intelligence, build stronger relationships, and better understand yourself and others.

Cultivate Compassion: Techniques for Self and Others

Definition: Compassion is more than just a feeling; it's an active desire to alleviate suffering.

It involves recognizing someone's pain and wanting to help. This extends beyond empathy, which is about feeling another's emotions, to taking action. It's crucial for personal growth because it fosters deeper connections and a sense of community.

Compassion isn't just for others; it's equally important to extend that same kindness and understanding to yourself. This dual focus on self and others creates a balanced approach to well-being.

Start with active listening and validation to practice compassion toward others.

- When someone shares their struggles, fully engage by making eye contact and nodding.

- Listen without interrupting and validate their feelings with phrases like, "That sounds really tough," or "I can see why you're upset."

- This simple act can make a big difference, showing you genuinely care.

Provide acts of kindness and service as a powerful way to cultivate compassion.

- This could be helping a neighbor with groceries or volunteering at a local shelter.

- These actions not only help others but also enrich your own sense of purpose and fulfillment.

Develop an attitude of non-judgment and acceptance.

- Try to approach each person and situation without preconceived notions.

- Accept others as they are, flaws and all, and recognize that everyone is fighting personal battles.

- Extend compassion to yourself. It can be more challenging, but it's equally vital.

Practice self-care and prioritize your needs.

- This might mean setting aside time each day for activities that rejuvenate you, whether reading a book, taking a walk, or simply relaxing.

Reframe negative self-talk with kind and supportive language.

- For example, instead of beating yourself up for a mistake, remind yourself that everyone makes errors and that they are opportunities to learn and grow.

- Engage in self-compassion exercises like loving-kindness meditation, which can be incredibly beneficial. This practice involves silently repeating phrases like, "May I be happy, may I be healthy, may I be at peace," to foster a sense of inner well-being and self-love.

Benefits

Cultivating compassion has numerous benefits for personal growth.

- It builds stronger, more empathic relationships.

- When you show genuine care and concern for others, they are more likely to reciprocate, creating a cycle of mutual support and understanding.

- Compassion also reduces stress and enhances emotional well-being.

- When you approach life with a compassionate mindset, you're more resilient in facing challenges.

- You understand that suffering is a part of the human experience, and you're better equipped to handle it.

- Additionally, fostering compassion brings a sense of inner peace and contentment.

- Knowing you're contributing positively to the world and treating yourself with kindness creates a deep sense of fulfillment.

Exercises

9H. To practice cultivating compassion, try incorporating these techniques into your daily routine.

- Start with active listening during conversations.

- Make a conscious effort to fully engage and validate the other person's feelings.

- Engage in acts of kindness, whether big or small, to positively impact those around you.

- Develop an attitude of non-judgment by reminding yourself that everyone has their own struggles.

- For self-compassion, prioritize self-care by scheduling time for activities that nurture you.

- Reframe negative self-talk with supportive language and try loving-kindness meditation to cultivate inner peace.

91. Loving-Kindness Meditation Exercise

- Find a quiet place where you won't be disturbed.

- Sit comfortably and close your eyes.

- Take a few deep breaths to center yourself.

- Silently repeat the following phrases: "May I be happy. May I be healthy. May I be at peace."

- After a few minutes, extend these wishes to others, starting with loved ones, then acquaintances, and finally, even those you find challenging: "May you be happy. May you be healthy. May you be at peace."

- This practice fosters compassion for yourself and others, creating a sense of interconnectedness and well-being.

Mindfulness and Empathy: Be Present with Yourself and Others

One afternoon, as I rushed through a busy day, my mind darted from one task to another. I was physically present but emotionally absent, missing the subtle cues and feelings of those around me. That's when I decided to try mindfulness.

Definition: Mindfulness is the practice of being fully present and aware in the moment.

It's about paying attention to your thoughts, feelings, and surroundings without judgment. This heightened awareness can significantly enhance empathy, allowing you to be tuned to your own and others' experiences.

Exercises

Mindfulness practices can seamlessly integrate into your daily life.

9J. One of the simplest methods is mindful breathing.

- Take a few moments each day to focus on your breath.
- Inhale deeply, feeling the air fill your lungs, and then exhale slowly.
- This practice centers and calms the mind, making it easier to connect with your emotions and the emotions of others.

9K. Another effective practice is the body scan meditation.

- Lie down or sit comfortably and slowly bring your attention to different parts of your body, from your toes to your head.
- Notice any sensations, tension, or discomfort.
- This exercise increases awareness of physical sensations, helping you stay present and grounded.

9L. Mindful observation is another valuable technique.

- Take a few minutes each day to observe your surroundings with full attention.
- Whether you watch the leaves rustle in the wind or listen to the sounds of your neighborhood, this practice enhances your attentiveness to details you might otherwise overlook.
- It sharpens your senses and deepens your connection to the world around you, enhancing your ability to empathize with others.

Benefits

The benefits of mindfulness for personal growth are profound.

- Improved emotional regulation is one of the key advantages.

- When you are mindful, you become more aware of your emotional responses, allowing you to manage stress and react more calmly to challenging situations.

- This emotional stability enhances self-awareness and self-understanding as you gain insights into your patterns of thought and behavior.

- Moreover, mindfulness fosters a greater ability to connect with others more deeply. Being fully present allows you to listen more intently, understand more deeply, and respond empathetically.

Exercises

9M. Try guided meditations to practice mindfulness and enhance empathy. These meditations often involve visualizing yourself in someone else's situation and feeling their emotions.

9N. Reflective journaling on mindfulness experiences and insights is another effective practice.

- After a mindfulness session, jot down your thoughts and feelings.

- Reflect on how being present affected your emotional state and interactions.

9O. Practicing mindful listening in conversations is also crucial.

- When someone speaks to you, focus entirely on their words and emotions, setting aside your thoughts and distractions.

- This deep listening enhances connection and understanding.

Imagine sitting with a friend who is sharing a personal struggle. Instead of planning your response or getting lost in your thoughts, you fully engage in the moment. You listen to their words, notice their body language, and feel their emotions. This mindful presence deepens your connection and shows your friend you genuinely care. It's a powerful way to build empathy and strengthen your relationships.

Overcome Emotional Exhaustion: Strategies for Renewal

I remember a time when I felt utterly drained as if I were running on fumes. The constant emotional demands of work, family, and life had taken their toll, leaving me overwhelmed and physically depleted.

- Emotional exhaustion is more than just feeling tired; it's a deep sense of being emotionally spent.

- It's that feeling when you have nothing left to give and your energy reserves are empty.

- This state can significantly impact your well-being, reducing emotional and physical energy.

- You may find it hard to engage in activities you once enjoyed, and even simple tasks can feel insurmountable.

Action Items

One effective method for overcoming emotional exhaustion is engaging in therapeutic activities.

- Nature walks, for example, offer a peaceful escape from the hustle and bustle of daily life. The fresh air, the sound of birds, and the beauty of the natural world can rejuvenate your spirit.

- Creative hobbies like painting, knitting, or playing an instrument can also provide a much-needed outlet for stress. These activities allow you to focus on something enjoyable and fulfilling, allowing your emotions to recover.

Another powerful strategy is practicing relaxation techniques.

- Deep breathing exercises, where you inhale slowly through your nose and exhale through your mouth, can instantly calm your nervous system.

- Progressive muscle relaxation, which involves tensing and relaxing different muscle groups, can also help release physical tension and promote a sense of calm.

Setting boundaries is crucial to reducing emotional overload.

- Saying "no" without guilt can protect your energy and prevent burnout.

- It's about recognizing your limits and honoring them.

- This might mean declining an extra project at work or setting aside time each day for yourself.

- Boundaries create a safe space to recharge and maintain your emotional well-being.

Benefits

Addressing emotional exhaustion restores your energy and enhances your overall well-being.

- When you overcome this depletion, you build emotional resilience, equipping you to handle future stressors.

- This resilience leads to improved emotional stability, allowing you to navigate life's ups and downs with greater ease.

Additionally, overcoming emotional exhaustion enhances your quality of life.

- You'll have more energy to fully engage in personal and professional pursuits.

- Activities that once felt like a chore will become enjoyable again, and you'll be able to connect more deeply with others.

Exercises

9P. To practice emotional renewal, start by creating a personal renewal plan.

- List your favorite restorative activities and schedule time for them regularly.
- This plan serves as a reminder to prioritize your well-being.

9Q. Journaling reflections on emotional triggers and renewal strategies is another effective practice.

- Write about what drains your energy and explore ways to mitigate these stressors.
- Reflect on the activities that help you feel renewed and incorporate them into your routine.

9R. Practicing self-compassion and self-care routines is also vital.

- Treat yourself with the same kindness and understanding that you would offer a friend.
- This might include simple acts like taking a warm bath, enjoying a cup of tea, or spending time with loved ones.

By integrating these strategies into your life, you can overcome emotional exhaustion and create a foundation of emotional resilience and stability. These practices restore your energy and enhance your overall well-being, allowing you to engage more fully in all aspects of your life.

Empathic Journaling: Write for Personal Insight

One quiet evening, I sat by the window, my journal in hand, reflecting on the day's events. I started writing about a conversation with a colleague who seemed unusually distant. As I wrote, I tried to put myself in their shoes, considering what might be happening in their life.

This exercise of empathic journaling opened up a new dimension of understanding. It wasn't just about recounting events but about exploring emotions, thoughts, and experiences with compassion. Empathic journaling involves writing with empathy toward oneself and others. It's a way to delve into your feelings and reactions, aiming to understand them without judgment.

To start with empathic journaling, consider using prompts focusing on empathy and self-reflection.

- For example, you might begin by asking, "What emotions did I experience today, and why?" This will help you explore the root of your feelings.

Another powerful technique is writing letters of compassion to yourself or others.

- Imagine writing a letter to yourself after a particularly tough day, offering encouragement and understanding.
- Or write to someone else, expressing empathy for their struggles.

Reflecting on daily interactions and emotional responses is also key.

- After a significant interaction, jot down your feelings and thoughts.
- What did you learn about yourself and the other person?

Benefits

The benefits of empathic journaling for personal growth are substantial.

- Regularly engaging in this practice gives you deeper insights into your emotions and behaviors.
- You start to notice patterns and triggers, which enhances your self-awareness.

- This self-understanding naturally extends to others, enhancing your empathy and ability to connect.

- Empathic journaling fosters a sense of inner peace and emotional balance.

- When you write with compassion, you create a safe space to explore your feelings, which can be incredibly soothing and grounding.

Exercises

9S. To practice empathic journaling, try incorporating daily prompts focused on empathy and compassion.

- For example, ask yourself, "How did I show empathy today?" or "What could I have done differently to be more compassionate?"

- These prompts guide your reflections and deepen your understanding.

9T. Reflective exercises on past experiences and lessons learned are also valuable.

- Think back to a challenging situation and write about how you handled it.

- What did you learn? How can you apply this insight moving forward?

9U. Writing gratitude journals is another excellent practice.

- Each day, note down things you are grateful for, focusing on moments of kindness and empathy.

- This positive focus can shift your mindset and cultivate a sense of appreciation.

One evening, after a difficult week, I was feeling particularly low. I decided to write a letter to myself, acknowledging my efforts and offering words of kindness. As I wrote, I felt a weight lift off my shoulders. This act of self-compassion was incredibly healing.

Writing letters of compassion, whether to yourself or others, can be a transformative exercise. It allows you to articulate empathy and kindness, reinforcing these qualities in your life.

Empathic journaling is not just about recording events; it's about engaging with your inner world compassionately and with understanding. Making this practice a regular part of your routine can enhance your self-awareness, deepen your empathy, and foster emotional balance. This simple yet profound tool can lead to significant personal growth, helping you navigate life with greater insight and compassion.

Adopt Empathy Long-term: Recommended Books, Apps, and Support Groups

Books can be a great source of wisdom and practical advice. If you're looking to delve deeper into empathy and related topics, several excellent titles can help.

Books

- **The Empath's Survival Guide** by Judith Orloff is a must-read. It offers practical tools for empaths to protect their energy and navigate the complexities of life with heightened sensitivity. Orloff's insights are grounded in her professional expertise and personal experiences, making it engaging and relatable.

- **Dare to Lead** by Brené Brown is another fantastic book. Brown explores the intersection of empathy, vulnerability, and leadership. She provides actionable strategies for leading with empathy and courage. Her writing is inspiring and practical, making it a valuable resource for anyone looking to integrate empathy into their leadership style.

- **Emotional Intelligence** by Daniel Goleman is a classic that delves into the science of emotional intelligence and its impact on our lives. Goleman's work is foundational for understanding how empathy fits into the broader scope of emotional intelligence, providing both scientific insights and practical applications.

Apps

In today's digital age, apps can be valuable tools for developing empathy.

- **Headspace** is an excellent app with guided meditations focused on empathy and compassion. With various courses and single sessions, it offers something for everyone, whether you're new to meditation or a seasoned practitioner. The app's user-friendly interface makes incorporating mindfulness into your daily routine easy.

- **Calm** is another fantastic app that offers mindfulness practices and relaxation techniques. It includes guided meditations, sleep stories, and breathing exercises to reduce stress and enhance emotional well-being. It's a great resource for building a daily mindfulness practice.

- **Insight Timer** provides a wide range of meditation and mindfulness resources, including thousands of free guided meditations. The app also features community groups to connect with others on similar journeys, adding a social support element to your practice.

Support Groups

Joining support groups can offer additional guidance and community for empathic individuals.

- **Online forums and communities for empaths** are abundant and can be incredibly supportive. These platforms provide a space to share experiences, offer advice, and receive encouragement from those who understand what you're going through. Look for groups on social media platforms like Facebook or specialized forums dedicated to empathy and emotional intelligence.

- **Local support groups and meetups** can also be invaluable. These gatherings provide face-to-face interaction and a sense of community. Whether you're attending a workshop, a book club focused on empathy or a casual meetup, these interactions can offer real-time support and shared experiences. Start by searching for local meetups on platforms like

Meetup.com. Many groups are dedicated to mindfulness, empathy, and emotional intelligence.

- **Professional counseling and therapy groups** specializing in empathy and emotional intelligence can provide more structured support. Therapists and counselors trained in these areas can offer targeted advice and coping strategies, making them a valuable resource for those struggling with empathy-related challenges.

Finding and joining support groups is easier than you might think. Joining online communities on social media can also connect you with like-minded individuals. Don't hesitate to seek referrals from therapists or counselors, as they often know about local and online groups that can provide the support you need.

Summary Points

By leveraging these resources, you can deepen your understanding of empathy and find the support you need to navigate life's challenges. Whether through books, apps, or support groups, these tools can help you cultivate a more empathetic and connected life.

As we look ahead, the next chapter will focus on applying empathy in various contexts, from personal relationships to professional settings, offering practical techniques for making empathy an integral part of daily life.

CHAPTER 10

EXPLORE INTERACTIVE EXERCISES AND PRACTICAL APPLICATIONS

P icture this: you're sitting in a quiet room, holding a mug of a hot beverage, contemplating your interactions over the past week. You recall moments where you felt deeply connected to others and times when you felt disconnected. You wonder why some conversations flowed effortlessly while others felt strained. This reflection sparks a desire to understand your empathic abilities better. At this point, consider taking a self-assessment quiz, a tool designed to help you gain insights into your strengths and areas for improvement in empathy. This quiz is included in the bonus supplement of illustrations, quizzes and forms for this book.

SELF-ASSESSMENT QUIZ: DISCOVER YOUR EMPATHIC STRENGTHS

The purpose of this self-assessment quiz is to offer you a mirror into your empathic self. It helps you identify your strengths, recognize areas for growth, and understand your personal empathic abilities. Empathy isn't a one-size-fits-all trait; it varies in depth and expression from person to person. This quiz will guide you in discovering where you stand and how you can enhance your empathic skills.

Answer Key: Hardly Ever – 1   Not Often – 2   Sometimes – 3   Frequently – 4   Almost Always – 5

Emotional Awareness: Understanding personal empathic abilities starts with self-awareness. Recognizing your emotional landscape is the first step in becoming more empathic.

1. _____ How often do you notice your own emotions as they arise?

2. _____ Do you acknowledge them, or do they pass by unnoticed, like background noise?

3. _____ How often do you tune into your own emotional state throughout the day?

4. _____ Do you take time to reflect on your emotional responses to different situations?

Emotional Awareness Total Score: _____

Perspective Taking: The perspective you take is another crucial aspect of empathy. It involves stepping into someone else's shoes to understand their viewpoint.

5. _____ How easily can you see the world from another person's perspective?

6. _____ Do you find it natural, or do you struggle to shift your viewpoint?

7. _____ How easily can you understand others' viewpoints, even if they differ from your own?

8. _____ Can you empathize with someone's feelings if you haven't had the same experiences?

Perspective Taking Total Score: _____

Empathic Listening: Listening empathically is the ability to truly hear and understand what others say verbally and emotionally.

9. _____ Do people often come to you for advice or support?

10. _____ Are you the go-to person for friends and family when they need someone to listen?

11. _____ Do people frequently seek your advice and support?

12. _____ Are you comfortable with listening and not immediately offering solutions?

Emotional Awareness Total Score: _____

Once you've completed the quiz, interpreting the results will provide valuable insights. Actionable steps based on your quiz results will guide your personal development.

High Scores

High scores of 16 – 20 in each area of emotional awareness, perspective-taking, and empathic listening indicate strong empathic abilities. These strengths are your foundation, the skills you can rely on and continue to develop.

Those with high scores should aim to maintain and refine these abilities.

- Engage in practices that challenge and expand your empathic skills, such as advanced active listening exercises or volunteering in diverse communities.

Lower Scores

Don't be disheartened if you find lower scores of 4 – 12 in any of these areas. These scores aren't permanent; they simply highlight where you can focus your efforts to grow.

For areas where you scored lower, specific exercises and practices can help strengthen these weak spots.

- If **emotional awareness** is an area for growth, consider daily reflection or mindfulness practices to become more attuned to your emotions.

- If **perspective-taking** is challenging, read books or watch films that offer different cultural or personal perspectives.

- If you need to improve **empathic listening**, practice listening to others without interjecting your own experiences, focusing entirely on their narrative.

This self-assessment quiz is a step toward becoming more empathic and connected with yourself and others. It's a tool that offers clarity and direction, empowering you to enhance your empathy in meaningful ways. As you engage with the quiz and reflect on your results, you'll find a path that leads to deeper connections and a more empathetic life.

Empathy Exercises for Daily Practice: Build Your Skills

Developing empathy is not a one-time event but an ongoing practice. Making empathy a regular part of your daily routine helps to build it as a habit, enhancing your interactions and relationships. Think of it like physical fitness; just as you wouldn't expect to stay in shape by going to the gym once a month, you can't expect to maintain empathic abilities without consistent practice. Regular empathy exercises help you stay emotionally aware and connected, making navigating the complexities of human relationships easier.

Exercises

10A. One of the most effective ways to practice empathy is through active listening. This means giving your full attention to the person speaking without interrupting or planning your response while they talk.

- Start by practicing with family or friends.

- When someone shares something with you, make a conscious effort to listen deeply.

- Nod along, make eye contact, and use affirming phrases like "I see" or "That sounds challenging."

- After they finish, reflect on what you heard to ensure you understood them correctly.

- This shows you care and deepens your understanding of their feelings and perspectives.

10B. Reflecting on your daily interactions can also help you identify moments of empathy and areas for improvement.

- At the end of each day, take a few minutes to think about your conversations.

- Were there moments where you felt particularly connected to someone?

- Were there times when you missed an opportunity to be empathic?

- Write these reflections down in a journal.

- Over time, try to notice patterns and gain insights into how you can enhance your empathy in future interactions.

- This practice increases self-awareness and helps you learn from your experiences.

10C. Engaging in random acts of kindness is another powerful way to build empathy.

- Simple gestures like holding the door for someone, complimenting a colleague, or sending a thoughtful message to a friend can make a big difference.

- These acts of kindness shift your focus from yourself to others, fostering a sense of connection and compassion.

- They also create a ripple effect, encouraging others to act kindly in return, transforming your social environment into a more empathetic space.

Benefits

Consistent empathy practice brings numerous benefits.

- First, it improves your emotional awareness and regulation. By regularly tuning into your own emotions and the emotions of others, you become more adept at managing your feelings and responding to others in a balanced way.

- This heightened emotional intelligence makes it easier to navigate complex social dynamics and reduces stress in your interactions.

- Additionally, consistent empathy practice strengthens relationships. Understanding and validating others' feelings fosters trust and intimacy, making relationships more resilient and fulfilling.

The overall well-being and satisfaction you gain from these practices can be profound.

- Feeling connected and understood by others enhances your sense of belonging and happiness.

- It also creates a positive feedback loop; the more empathy you practice, the more rewarding your interactions become, encouraging you to continue developing these skills.

Action Items

- Set aside dedicated time daily to integrate empathy exercises into your daily life. This could be as simple as spending five minutes in the morning reflecting on how you'll practice empathy that day or ending your day with a brief journaling session.

- Use reminders and prompts to stay consistent. Sticky notes on your bathroom mirror, calendar alerts, or even a dedicated empathy journal can help you remember to practice.

- Tracking your progress and reflections in a journal can be particularly beneficial. Note your daily empathy exercises and interactions and what you learned from them. This will keep you accountable and allow you to see your growth over time.

Making empathy a regular part of your routine transforms it from an abstract concept into a tangible skill. By actively listening, reflecting on your interactions, engaging in acts of kindness, and consistently practicing empathy, you create a life enriched with deeper connections and greater emotional understanding.

Role-Playing Scenarios: Practice Empathic Responses

Imagine sitting in a room with a close friend who has been through a rough patch. They're visibly upset, and you want to comfort them but aren't sure how to begin. Role-playing can be an invaluable tool for practicing these kinds of empathic responses.

Simulating real-life interactions can help you build your skills and gain confidence in empathic communication. Think of it as a rehearsal for real-life scenarios, allowing you to try different approaches and learn what works best without the pressure of an emotional crisis.

Exercises

10D. One helpful scenario to practice with a partner is comforting a friend going through a tough time.

- Start by having one person play the role of the friend in distress while the other practices offering support.

- Focus on maintaining eye contact, using a soothing tone, and validating their feelings.

- You might say, "I can see how much this is hurting you, and I'm here for you."

- This exercise helps you refine your ability to provide emotional support without jumping to solutions or minimizing their feelings.

10E. Another valuable scenario to practice with 3 people is mediating a conflict between colleagues at work.

- In this role-play, assign roles such as the conflicting parties and the mediator.

- The mediator's job is to listen to both sides, acknowledge their feelings, and guide them toward a resolution.

- You can practice phrases like, "I understand that you're frustrated because you feel overlooked, and I appreciate you sharing that."

- This scenario helps you develop the skills to manage conflict empathetically, fostering a more harmonious work environment.

10F. Another critical scenario is listening to a partner express their feelings about a disagreement.

- In this exercise, one person shares their feelings about a recent argument, and the other practices active listening and empathic responses.

- You might say, "I hear that you felt ignored during our conversation, and I'm sorry for that. Let's talk about how we can communicate better."

- This role-play helps you practice navigating disagreements with empathy, improving your relationship dynamics.

For effective role-playing, use realistic and relatable scenarios. Choose situations you will likely encounter, such as comforting a friend, mediating workplace conflicts, or listening to your partner. Practicing with a partner or group can also provide diverse perspectives and enrich the experience. Different people bring unique insights and suggestions, helping you see the situation from various angles.

Reflecting on the experience and identifying lessons learned is crucial. After each role-play, take a moment to discuss and reflect. What did you learn? How did it feel to give and receive empathy? What would you do differently next time?

Benefits

Practicing in a safe environment, like role-playing, offers several benefits.

- First, it builds your confidence and competence in empathic interactions. Rehearsing different scenarios makes you more comfortable and adept at responding empathetically in real-life situations.

- Second, it provides an opportunity to receive feedback and identify areas for improvement. After each role-play, discuss what went well and what could be improved. This feedback helps you refine your approach and enhance your empathic skills.

- Third, role-playing enhances emotional regulation and response skills. By simulating challenging interactions, you learn to manage your emotions and respond thoughtfully rather than reactively.

Role-playing is a powerful tool for enhancing empathy. By simulating real-life scenarios, you can build your skills, gain confidence, and improve your ability to respond with empathy in various situations. Whether comforting a friend, mediating conflicts at work, or navigating disagreements in your relationships, role-playing helps you practice and refine your empathic responses, making you more adept at connecting with others on a deeper level.

Guided Meditations for Empaths: Find Inner Peace

Imagine coming home after a long day, your mind buzzing with the emotions and energies you've absorbed from others. You feel overwhelmed as if you're carrying the weight of the world on your shoulders.

This is a common experience for empaths, who often struggle to find balance amidst the emotional chaos. Guided meditations can be a lifeline, helping you find inner peace and emotional equilibrium. These meditations not only calm the mind but also reduce stress, enhance self-awareness, and improve emotional regulation.

Exercises

10G. Guided meditations for grounding and centering are particularly beneficial.

- Start by sitting comfortably and closing your eyes.

- Focus on your breath, feeling the rise and fall of your chest.

- Imagine roots growing from the soles of your feet, anchoring you to the earth.

- With each breath, feel the stability and strength of these roots, grounding you in the present moment.

- This meditation helps you stay centered, preventing the emotional whirlwind from sweeping you away. It's a powerful way to reclaim your sense of stability and calm.

10H. Another type of guided meditation is loving-kindness meditation, which focuses on sending compassion to yourself and others. (Note: This exercise was in chapter 9 for compassion, and it's repeated here for empaths.)

- Begin by sitting quietly and taking a few deep breaths.

- Picture yourself surrounded by a warm, loving light.

- Silently repeat phrases like, "May I be happy, may I be healthy, may I be at peace."

- After a few minutes, extend these wishes to others: first to loved ones, then to acquaintances, and finally to those with whom you have difficulties.

- This practice fosters a sense of connection and compassion, enhancing your ability to empathize with others while also nurturing self-compassion.

10I. Visualization meditation is another excellent tool for empaths. This practice involves imagining a peaceful and safe place where you can retreat mentally whenever you need a break.

- Close your eyes and take a few deep breaths.

- Visualize a serene location, such as a tranquil beach, a quiet forest, or a cozy room.

- Imagine every detail—the sound of waves, the scent of pine, the warmth of a fireplace.

- Spend a few minutes in this mental sanctuary, allowing yourself to relax and recharge.

- Visualization meditation can be a refuge from the emotional demands of daily life, offering a moment of peace and rejuvenation.

Benefits

The benefits of regular meditation practice are far-reaching.

- Guided meditations reduce emotional overload and burnout, a common issue for empaths who constantly absorb others' emotions. By meditating each day, you create a buffer against this emotional overwhelm.

- Meditation also improves focus and concentration, making it easier to navigate complex social dynamics and maintain emotional balance.

- Over time, regular meditation enhances overall mental and emotional health, contributing to a more resilient and centered self.

Action Items

Set aside dedicated time each day to integrate meditation into your daily routine. Consistency is key, whether it's five minutes in the morning or twenty minutes before bed.

Create a comfortable and quiet space for your practice. This could be a corner of your bedroom with a cushion and a blanket or a spot in your living room with a comfy chair and soft lighting. The environment you create should invite relaxation and focus, free from distractions.

Using guided meditation apps or recordings can provide additional support.

- Apps like **Insight Timer** and **Calm** offer a variety of guided meditations tailored to different needs, from grounding and centering to loving-kindness and visualization.

- These resources can be particularly helpful if you're new to meditation or prefer guided sessions over meditating on your own. They offer structure and guidance, making it easier to stick with your practice and experience its benefits.

Guided meditations can transform the way you navigate your emotional landscape. By calming the mind, reducing stress, and enhancing self-awareness, these practices help you find balance and peace amidst chaos. As you incorporate meditation into your routine, you'll likely find yourself better equipped to handle emotional challenges, more attuned to your needs, and more connected to the world around you.

Worksheets to Set Boundaries: Practical Tools for Implementation

Imagine this: you're at the end of another exhausting day, feeling like your boundaries have been trampled over by everyone from your boss to your closest friend. You know you need to set firmer boundaries, but you're unsure where to start.

This is where boundary-setting worksheets come into play.

- Boundary-setting worksheets offer structured guidance, helping you implement and maintain boundaries effectively.

- These worksheets encourage self-reflection, allowing you to identify what you need and why those needs are crucial.

- They also aid in planning, giving you a roadmap for conversations and strategies to uphold your limits.

Exercises

Make your own worksheets or copy the worksheets included in the book at the end of this chapter.

10J. The **Identifying Personal Boundaries Worksheet** is one of the most valuable worksheets. This worksheet prompts you to reflect on past experiences and current needs.
Part 1:

- For example, think about times when you felt overwhelmed or taken advantage of.

- By jotting down these reflections, you gain clarity on occasions when your boundaries are weakest.

- What patterns do you notice? Perhaps you find it challenging to refuse family requests, or your work-life balance suffers because you're always accessible to your employer.

Part 2:

- Use the patterns to define when and where boundaries are needed.

- This self-awareness is the first step in fortifying your emotional defenses.

10K. Another essential tool is the **Planning Boundary-Setting Conversations Worksheet**. This tool helps you prepare scripts and strategies, making these often tricky discussions more manageable.

- For example, suppose you need to set a boundary with a demanding colleague. In that case, the worksheet might guide you to script a conversation that starts with an "I" statement, such as, "I feel overwhelmed when work tasks spill into my personal time. I need to set a clear boundary that I am not available after 6 PM."

- This preparation boosts your confidence and ensures you communicate your needs effectively.

10L. The **Tracking Boundary Maintenance Worksheet** is equally important; this is where the third worksheet comes in. This worksheet allows you to record successes and challenges, providing a tangible record of your progress.

- Did you manage to say no to an unreasonable request this week? Write it down.

- Did you struggle to enforce a boundary with a friend? Note that too.

- As you keep this log, notice your growth over time and identify patterns that need more attention.

- This ongoing reflection helps you stay accountable and consistent in maintaining your boundaries.

Benefits

The benefits of using these structured tools are manifold.

- First, they increase clarity and confidence in boundary-setting. A clear plan and a script make you less likely to be swayed by guilt or pressure.

- Second, these worksheets provide a tangible record of your progress and growth. Seeing your successes written down can be incredibly affirming and motivating.

- Finally, they encourage accountability and consistency. Regularly revisiting and updating your worksheets ensures that boundary-setting becomes a sustained practice, not a one-time effort.

Action Items

To use these worksheets effectively, set aside regular time for these activities. It could be a quiet Sunday afternoon or a few minutes each evening. The key is consistency.

Reflect honestly and thoroughly on the prompts. This isn't about getting the "right" answers but better understanding yourself. Be candid in your reflections, even if it's uncomfortable.

Review and update the worksheets as needed based on your experiences. Life is dynamic, and so are your boundaries. As you grow and change, so will your needs. Regular updates ensure your boundaries remain relevant and effective.

Worksheets

Samples of each of the worksheets described above are shown on the following pages. Whether you copy them or make your own, recognize them as an optional tool to facilitate exercises 10J, 10K and 10L.

IDENTIFY PERSONAL BOUNDARIES
WORKSHEET – PART 1 ©

Write about instances when you felt overwhelmed, taken advantage of, unappreciated, or resentful.

- When and where was this? What were the circumstances? How did you respond?
- Which of these feelings did you experience?
- Reflecting on these incidents, what patterns can you identify? For example, you said "yes" when you wanted to say "no," repeated interruptions during personal time, or inconsiderate requests that you do more.

Situation	My Feelings	Pattern Identified

Identify Personal Boundaries
Worksheet – Part 2 ©

Based on the situations recorded, write down what boundaries are needed.
- What scenario makes you uncomfortable or stressed?
- What boundary do you want to set for this?

Scenario	Boundary Needed

Plan Boundary-Setting Conversations
WORKSHEET ©

Write a script for communicating each boundary, using the boundaries you identified on the Identify Personal Boundaries Worksheet.

- Use "I" statements, not "you."
- Be serious and firm to avoid pushback.
- Reinforce that your boundaries are non-negotiable.
- Avoid mixed messages that suggest your boundary is flexible.
- Don't feel guilty about caring for your needs.

Scenario	Boundary Needed	Script

Track Boundary Maintenance
WORKSHEET ©

Write down when your boundary is resisted or violated and what you did to reinforce it.

Date	Boundary	Pushback Scenario	My Reinforcement Response

Summary Points

Boundary-setting worksheets are practical tools that offer structure and support in maintaining personal limits. By identifying boundaries, planning conversations, and tracking progress, these worksheets help you build a solid foundation for emotional well-being. They provide the clarity, confidence, and consistency needed to protect your energy and maintain healthy relationships.

As you integrate these tools into your routine, you'll find yourself more empowered and better equipped to navigate the complexities of boundary-setting.

Conclusion

As we reach the end of this journey together, I want to reflect on the key themes and objectives we've explored. We began by understanding the profound difference empathy can make in our connections with others. Through personal stories, practical techniques, and scientific insights, we've delved into the many facets of empathy and how it can transform our lives.

Empathic communication is at the heart of this book. It's more than just listening, whether in person or virtual; it's about truly understanding and sharing another person's feelings. Empathy allows for deeper, more meaningful connections, whether you're comforting a friend, resolving a workplace conflict, or simply engaging in everyday conversations. It builds trust, fosters mutual respect, and creates a supportive environment where everyone feels valued.

We've also explored the importance of **understanding diverse perspectives**. Learning about other cultures and stepping into someone else's shoes can break down biases and prejudices, fostering a more inclusive and respectful world. This skill is crucial not just in personal relationships but also in professional settings. It enhances teamwork, innovation, and problem-solving by bringing multiple viewpoints to collaboration.

Self-empathy and self-care are equally vital. In our fast-paced world, it's easy to neglect our own emotional needs. But treating yourself with the same kindness and understanding you offer others is essential for maintaining emotional balance and resilience. Through daily self-care practices, mindfulness, and grounding techniques, you can nurture your well-being and build a strong foundation for empathy towards others.

Building emotional resilience is another key theme. Life is full of challenges, and bouncing back from setbacks with strength and grace is a valuable skill. By practicing gratitude, connecting with others, and engaging in activities that boost resilience, you can enhance your overall well-being and navigate life's ups and downs with greater ease.

Setting healthy boundaries is crucial for protecting your energy and maintaining emotional stability. Whether dealing with a demanding boss, a manipulative friend, or an overbearing family member, clear and firm boundaries ensure your needs are respected. This book has provided practical steps and scripts for setting and maintaining boundaries without guilt, helping you foster healthier relationships and prevent burnout.

Empathy in leadership is a powerful tool for creating supportive and productive work environments. An empathic leader listens, understands, and cares for their team members, fostering trust, collaboration, and innovation. By integrating empathy into decision-making and daily interactions, leaders can build stronger, more resilient teams and drive positive organizational change.

Navigating difficult relationships, especially with empathy-deficient individuals, requires unique strategies. We've discussed techniques for protecting your energy, staying grounded, and setting boundaries with narcissists, sociopaths, and psychopaths. These skills are essential for maintaining your emotional well-being and ensuring you don't get drained by toxic interactions.

Empathy in the digital age faces new challenges. Virtual meetings, social media, and constant connectivity can make genuine human connection more difficult. But you can maintain empathy even in a digitally saturated world by practicing empathic communication in virtual settings, engaging in positive interactions on social media, and balancing online presence with emotional well-being through digital detoxes.

Throughout this book, we've emphasized the importance of ongoing practice through interactive exercises and practical applications. From self-assessment quizzes to empathy exercises, role-playing scenarios, guided meditations, and boundary-setting worksheets, these tools are designed to help you integrate empathy into your daily life. They provide a structured way to practice and refine your empathic skills, ensuring you continue growing and developing.

So, what's the next step? I encourage you to apply the insights, techniques, and exercises from this book to your everyday interactions. Practice active listening, engage in perspective-taking, set and maintain healthy boundaries, and nurture your well-being through self-care and mindfulness. Use empathy as a guiding principle in your personal and professional life, and watch as it transforms your relationships and enhances your overall well-being.

Remember, empathy is not just a skill; it's a way of being. It's about connecting with others on a deeper level, understanding their emotions, and responding with kindness and compassion. By embracing empathy, you contribute to a more understanding, supportive, and connected world.

Thank you for joining me on this journey. I hope that **Empathy Unlocked - Learning to Connect in a Disconnected World** has inspired you and provided you with valuable tools for building empathy. Together, we can create a world where empathy thrives and meaningful connections are the norm. Keep practicing, keep growing, and keep connecting with empathy.

Warm regards,
Delia Sikes

Review Request

Your voice is powerful. Many people decide which books to read based on recommendations like yours. That's why I'm asking you to leave a review for **Empathy Unlocked – Learning to Connect in a Disconnected World**. Leaving a review is a small, simple act that takes less than a minute but can profoundly impact someone's life.

Ready to share some kindness? It's easy! Just go to this book in Goodreads or on the website for the company from which you purchased the book, and leave your review with a rating, a video or photo, and your thoughts.

Remember that sharing knowledge is one of the best ways to extend empathy. If this book has touched you, consider passing it on to someone else who might benefit from it.

More Books by Delia Sikes

Please check out our companion book, **Overthinking – The Silent Saboteur**, or the combination book, **Empathy and Overthinking – Navigating Your Inner and Interpersonal Worlds**.

Please also check out Delia's book, **I'm Not Toxic, You're Overreacting**.

REFERENCES

Mirror Neurons, Empathy, and the Other
https://oxfordre.com/psychology/display/10.1093/acrefore/9780190236557.001.0001/acrefore-9780190236557-e-605

Sympathy vs. Empathy: What's the Difference?
https://www.verywellmind.com/sympathy-vs-empathy-whats-the-difference-7496474

Empathy development from adolescence to adulthood and ...
https://www.frontiersin.org/journals/psychology/articles/10.3389/fpsyg.2022.936053/full

Empathy across cultures – one size does not fit all
https://www.ncbi.nlm.nih.gov/pmc/articles/PMC9491267/

7 Active Listening Techniques For Better Communication
https://www.verywellmind.com/what-is-active-listening-3024343

Reflective Listening
https://www.maxwell.syr.edu/docs/default-source/ektron-files/reflective-listening-neil-katz-and-kevin-mcnulty.pdf?sfvrsn=f1fa6672_7

How to Understand Body Language and Facial Expressions
https://www.verywellmind.com/understand-body-language-and-facial-expressions-4147228

Empathy in the Digital Age
https://www.kornferry.com/insights/this-week-in-leadership/emotional-intelligence-empathy-digital-age

Developing Empathy: How to Strengthen Perspective Taking ...
https://everydayspeech.com/blog-posts/general/developing-empathy-how-to-strengthen-perspective-taking-skills/

Cultural Sensitivity in Communication - Day Translations Blog
https://www.daytranslations.com/blog/cultural-sensitivity-in-communication/

The Power of Empathy in Conflict Resolution - LinkedIn
https://www.linkedin.com/pulse/power-empathy-conflict-resolution-sarah-morgan#:~:text=Empathy%20helps%20prevent%20misunderstandings%20from,from%20spiraling%20out%20of%20control.

How Stories Change the Brain - Greater Good Science Center
https://greatergood.berkeley.edu/article/item/how_stories_change_brain

The power of self-compassion - Harvard Health
https://www.health.harvard.edu/healthbeat/the-power-of-self-compassion#:~:text=Self%2Dcompassion%20offers%20several%20benefits,their%20anxiety%20and%20related%20depression.

12 Self-Care Coping Skills for Empaths or HSP to Prevent ...
https://courageousandmindful.com/12-self-care-coping-skills-for-empaths-or-hsp-to-prevent-burn-out/

Emotional regulation: Skills, exercises, and strategies
https://www.betterup.com/blog/emotional-regulation-skills

30 Grounding Techniques to Quiet Distressing Thoughts
https://www.healthline.com/health/grounding-techniques

12 Signs You Need Better Boundaries
https://www.positivemindworks.co/12-signs-you-need-better-boundaries/

How To Set Healthy Boundaries in Relationships
https://health.clevelandclinic.org/how-to-set-boundaries

5 Things to Know About Setting Boundaries
https://www.psychologytoday.com/intl/blog/modern-dating/202212/5-things-to-know-about-setting-boundaries

Why Boundaries at Work Are Essential
https://www.psychologytoday.com/gb/blog/living-better-with-boundaries/202212/why-boundaries-at-work-are-essential

Empathy Is The Most Important Leadership Skill According ...
https://www.forbes.com/sites/tracybrower/2021/09/19/empathy-is-the-most-important-leadership-skill-according-to-research/

The Importance of Empathy in the Workplace - CCL.org
https://www.ccl.org/articles/leading-effectively-articles/empathy-in-the-workplace-a-tool-for-effective-leadership/

Microsoft CEO Satya Nadella: How Empathy Sparks Innovation
https://knowledge.wharton.upenn.edu/article/microsofts-ceo-on-how-empathy-sparks-innovation/

Managing Stress: Four Key Strategies for Leaders
https://www.furstgroup.com/resources/managing-stress-five-key-strategies-for-leaders

Empathy in Remote Work: Connecting in a Disconnected ...
https://www.linkedin.com/pulse/empathy-remote-work-connecting-disconnected-world-bram-weerts

8 Ways Successful People Retain Their Empathy In A ...
https://www.forbes.com/sites/averyblank/2021/02/16/8-ways-successful-people-retain-their-empathy-in-a-virtual-working-world/

The Role of Social Media in Our Empathy Crisis
https://www.psychologytoday.com/us/blog/the-art-living-free/202207/the-role-social-media-in-our-empathy-crisis

Why a "Digital Detox" Will Benefit Your Overall Mental Health
https://www.goodrx.com/health-topic/mental-health/digital-detox

Narcissist vs. Sociopath vs. Psychopath: What's the Difference?
https://lauriehollmanphd.com/2020/05/18/narcissist-vs-sociopath-vs-psychopath-whats-the-difference/

14 Tips for How to Deal With a Narcissist - Choosing Therapy
https://www.choosingtherapy.com/deal-with-narcissist/

Coping with Sociopaths (Antisocial Personality Disorder)
https://psychcentral.com/pro/recovery-expert/2019/10/coping-with-sociopaths-antisocial-personality-disorder

Five Ways To Set Boundaries With Toxic People
https://www.forbes.com/councils/forbescoachescouncil/2020/01/31/five-ways-to-set-boundaries-with-toxic-people/

Can Self-Awareness Help You Be More Empathic?
https://greatergood.berkeley.edu/article/item/can_self_awareness_help_you_be_more_empathic

Compassion Cultivation Training - Stanford Medicine
https://med.stanford.edu/psychiatry/education/cme/cct.html

Effectiveness of mindfulness-based interventions on empathy
   https://www.ncbi.nlm.nih.gov/pmc/articles/PMC9632989/

How to Refuel When You're Feeling Emotionally Drained
   https://hbr.org/2020/04/how-to-refuel-when-youre-feeling-emotionally-drained

Empathy Quiz - Greater Good Science Center
   https://greatergood.berkeley.edu/quizzes/take_quiz/empathy

40 Empathy Activities \u0026 Worksheets for Students \u0026 Adults
   https://positivepsychology.com/kindness-activities-empathy-worksheets/

Building Empathy Skills: Practical Role Play Scenarios for ...
   https://everydayspeech.com/blog-posts/general/building-empathy-skills-practical-role-play-scenarios-for-learning-and-growth/

Empath Meditation | Michelle Chalfant
   https://insighttimer.com/michellechalfant/guided-meditations/empath-meditation

ChatGPT. (2024). ChatGPT GPT-4 [Software]. OpenAI.
   https://openai.com/chatgpt

www.ingramcontent.com/pod-product-compliance
Lightning Source LLC
Chambersburg PA
CBHW060502030426
42337CB00015B/1705